HEARING EARTH'S CALL

Ecology and Justice

An Orbis Series on Integral Ecology

Advisory Board Members
Mary Evelyn Tucker
John A. Grim
Leonardo Boff
Sean McDonagh

The Orbis Series on Integral Ecology publishes books seeking to integrate an understanding of Earth's interconnected life systems with sustainable social, political, and economic systems that enhance the Earth community. Books in the series concentrate on ways to

- Reexamine human–Earth relations in light of contemporary cosmological and ecological science.
- Develop visions of common life marked by ecological integrity and social justice.
- Expand on the work of those exploring such fields as integral ecology, climate justice, Earth law, ecofeminism, and animal protection.
- Promote inclusive participatory strategies that enhance the struggle of Earth's poor and oppressed for ecological justice.
- Deepen appreciation for dialogue within and among religious traditions on issues of ecology and justice.
- Encourage spiritual discipline, social engagement, and the transformation of religion and society toward these ends.

Viewing the present moment as a time for fresh creativity and inspired by the encyclical *Laudato Si'*, the series seeks authors who speak to ecojustice concerns and who bring into this dialogue perspectives from the Christian communities, from the world's religions, from secular and scientific circles, or from new paradigms of thought and action.

Advance Praise for
HEARING EARTH'S CALL

"Rodolfo Felices Luna writes Hearing Earth's Call 'out of a conviction that First John can speak to our times' (133), and he does so with exegetical precision and incisive passion. His systematic approach to the text unearths its original context then shines a light on its timeless demand for the faithful to nurture all our fellow beings right alongside all our shared creation. Attentive readers of all sorts will not come away unaffected, rather compelled to active faith in their lives."

—**Sherri Brown,** professor
New Testament, Creighton University

"In this sensitive study of John's First Letter, Rodolfo Felices Luna has brought together two critical issues for our time: the cry of the earth and the cry of the poor. The two cannot be separated. In Exodus 3, God speaks to Moses saying, 'I have heard their cry, I know their sufferings' (3:7). The moral imperative of 'life' resounds through these pages, demanding that we, too, hear the cry, know the suffering, and act."

—**Mary Coloe,** PBVM
professor emerita, University of Divinity
Box Hill, Bunurong Country, Australia

"This is a good read that raises important questions on current issues such as the inhuman treatment of disenfranchised people, global warming, and the large scale destruction of the planet. With reference to the use of 1 John in Catholic liturgies, Dr. Luna notes: 'However, unless a Bible study group is formed for breaking open the word of God, only the hearing takes place, not the sharing. I encourage you to make a move in this direction. We hear God's word not only in silence and prayer but also from others, in the sharing of faith' (15). This is an important call for a synodal-type sharing, listening, and community engagement. Given the great need for, inter alia, greater inclusivity and a deeper ecological awareness, Dr. Luna provides much needed encouragement for engagement with the text in a meaningful and life changing way. I readily recommend this work to all serious readers of the Bible, and to all who seek conversion in an integral way, that is, in a way that includes the embracing of otherness and the sustaining of the ecology." —**Bishop Sylvester David,** OMI
Archdiocese of Cape Town, South Africa

"Luna reads 1 John's promise of 'enduring life' as a call to work for and protect the Earth and her poor. He calls on us to cherish biological life as an expression and icon of the life promised to us in Jesus."

—**Mari Joerstad,** academic dean, associate professor Hebrew Bible, Vancouver School of Theology, Canada

"What does a short, ancient letter with no references to nature have to say in an age of ecological collapse and social injustice? In *Hearing Earth's Call: Life and Livelihood in First John,* Rodolfo Felices Luna uncovers a bold proclamation of life—enduring life that resists indifference, challenges systems of domination, and invites renewed fellowship with the poor and the Earth itself. Blending careful exegesis with contemporary ecological theology, this book offers a compelling vision of Christian discipleship grounded in love and truth that begets life and shared livelihood." —**Sébastien Doane,** Université Laval author, *Reading the Bible amid the Environmental Crisis*

"Clear, concise, and compelling, Luna offers an accessible guide to 1 John that blends exegetical insights with contemporary connections to our global context. Luna's all-inclusive understanding of life in 1 John calls readers to value the perspectives of the poor and marginalized, dislodging the false comfort of exploitation in order to inspire true life for the whole Earth." —**Alicia D. Myers,** associate professor New Testament, Baylor University; research fellow University of the Free State, Bloemfontein, South Africa

"I highly recommend this ground-breaking, accessible book, which will gift the reader with profound and challenging insights drawn from bringing solid studies on First John into dialogue with concern for the poor and the environment that is at the core of Christian faith in Scripture."

—**Kathleen P. Rushton,** RSM, independent researcher Ōtautahi Christchurch, Aotearoa New Zealand

HEARING EARTH'S CALL

Life and Livelihood in First John

Rodolfo Felices Luna

ORBIS BOOKS
Maryknoll, New York 10545

Founded in 1970, Orbis Books endeavors to publish works that enlighten the mind, nourish the spirit, and challenge the conscience. The publishing arm of the Maryknoll Fathers and Brothers, Orbis seeks to explore the global dimensions of the Christian faith and mission, to invite dialogue with diverse cultures and religious traditions, and to serve the cause of reconciliation and peace. The books published reflect the views of their authors and do not represent the official position of the Maryknoll Society. To learn more about Maryknoll and Orbis Books, please visit our website at www.orbisbooks.com.

Copyright © 2025 by Rodolfo Felices Luna

Published by Orbis Books, Box 302, Maryknoll, NY 10545-0302.

Scripture texts in this work are taken from the New American Bible, Revised Edition (NABRE), copyright © 2010, Confraternity of Christian Doctrine, Washington, D.C. and are used by permission of the copyright owner. All Rights Reserved. No part of the New American Bible may be reproduced in any form without permission in writing from the copyright owner.

All Vatican documents are available online at Vatican.va.

All rights reserved.

No part of this publication may be reproduced or transmitted in any form or by any means, electronic or mechanical, including photocopying, recording, or any information storage or retrieval system, without prior permission in writing from the publisher.

Queries regarding rights and permissions should be addressed to: Orbis Books, P.O. Box 302, Maryknoll, NY 10545-0302.

Manufactured in the United States of America

Library of Congress Cataloging-in-Publication Data

Names: Luna, Rodolfo Felices, 1969- author
Title: Hearing earth's call : life and livelihood in first John / Rodolfo
   Felices Luna.
Description: Maryknoll, NY : Orbis Books, [2025] | Series: Ecology and
   justice | Includes bibliographical references and index. | Summary:
   "Examines First John from a theological perspective of environmental and
   economic justice"—Provided by publisher.
Identifiers: LCCN 2025016442 (print) | LCCN 2025016443 (ebook) | ISBN
   9781626986336 paperback | ISBN 9798888660881 epub
Subjects: LCSH: Bible. Epistle of John, 1st—Criticism, interpretation,
   etc. | Bible. Epistle of John, 1st—Theology | Environmental
   justice—Biblical teaching | Human ecology—Biblical teaching
Classification: LCC BS2805.52 .L85 2025 (print) | LCC BS2805.52 (ebook) |
   DDC 227/.9406—dc23/eng/20250708
LC record available at https://lccn.loc.gov/2025016442
LC ebook record available at https://lccn.loc.gov/2025016443

*To the Poor who cannot afford to read
and to Earth's living creatures
who count on you and me doing so wisely*

Contents

	Foreword	ix
1	**Let Life Bring Joy to All**	1
	The Train of Thought in 1:1–4	2
	Life	7
	Fellowship	14
	Joy	22
2	**God's Light upon Us**	26
	The Train of Thought in 1:5–2:7	29
	Shedding Light on Our Brokenness	31
	Walking under God's Light	34
3	**The Times Are Changing**	38
	The Train of Thought in 2:8–17	40
	Do Not Love the World?	44
	A World on the Brink of Collapse	47
	To Set Our Hope in the Light	51
4	**Remaining True**	53
	The Train of Thought in 2:18–28	55
	The Last Hour	56
	When Many Leave	57
	Remaining True to Our Calling	63
5	**Becoming Who We Are Called to Be**	65
	The Train of Thought in 2:29–3:10	67

		Daughters and Sons of the Righteous	70
		Lawlessness Is the Fruit of Deceit	72
		God's Seed	74
6	**Opening Our Hearts**		**78**
		The Train of Thought in 3:11–23	80
		To Love after Jesus	82
		Life and Livelihood	87
		God Is Greater Than Our Hearts	89
7	**Discerning God's Spirit in All Flesh**		**91**
		The Train of Thought in 3:24–4:13	94
		Spirits at Work	98
		God's Spirit of Love	101
8	**Witnessing to God's Love**		**104**
		The Train of Thought in 4:14–5:10	106
		Water, Spirit, Blood	111
		Faith in God's Love	114
9	**Embracing the Fellowship of Life**		**119**
		The Train of Thought in 5:11–21	121
		The Mirage of Idolatry: Living the Good Life	124
		What We Do Know	128

Afterword	133
The Literary Structure of 1 John	135
Further Reading	143
Scripture Index	147
Index	155

Foreword

περὶ τοῦ λόγου τῆς ζωῆς
Concerning the word of life
1 John 1:1f

It Is All about Life

The good news that followers of Jesus Christ proclaim is a word about life. Whatever is of interest in the Christian religion tells the story of life, celebrates life, and promises life. People paid attention, embraced this word, and handed it over across the centuries onto us because each generation of witnesses found life in this word. A word that provides an enduring taste of life and bears the promise of life is worth remembering and passing on. Life is all that really matters.

This book is about life, as found at the core and purpose of the First Letter of John, a writing of the turn of the first century that has been received into the canon of the New Testament by Christians of all denominations. The author of the letter writes, from the beginning,

> For the life was made visible; we have seen it and testify to it and proclaim to you the eternal life that was with the Father and was made visible to us. (1 Jn 1:2)

The letter is thus a written proclamation of life, of the life that was with God the Father and was made accessible to us by the coming of the Son of God. Such divine life is called "eternal," a qualifier that merits some pondering in the course of this book. For now, let us take the expression at face value. Some previously invisible quality of life was finally made visible in the life, death, and resurrection of Jesus of Nazareth, according to John. That is Good News to share and to marvel at, and it becomes the main topic for John's work.

When the letter comes to a close, the author recapitulates:

> I write these things to you so that you may know that you have eternal life, you who believe in the name of the Son of God. (1 Jn 5:13)

First John is a letter about the disclosure of life and the assurance of life. Belief in Jesus, the Son of God, opens up a whole new realm of existence that somehow lay previously hidden, unavailable, untapped, coiled back in a promise:

> And this is the promise that he made us: eternal life. (1 Jn 2:25)

For us readers, First John holds the promise of disclosing to us what this life is about, when and where it can be found, and how one can enjoy life to the fullest, even during our fleeting years of mortal existence on this Earth. If this topic interests you, then delving into First John will be rewarding, and this reading guide of a book may help some on your quest.

For This Book to Matter at All

During Easter week of the year 407 of our era, St. Augustine, bishop of Hippo, preached ten homilies on First John. Delivered in Latin, they have come down to us through the manuscript tradition of the West and are readily available in modern language translations.¹ In them, Augustine marveled at the succinct presentation of the gospel of love that St. John had provided for the church, and he drew riches from the letter for the benefit of his flock. From then onward, many a scholar and pastor have published a commentary, a reading guide, or a study of the letter. The twentieth century saw an exponential rise in exegetical commentaries, putting to use modern linguistic, historical, and rhetorical tools to shed light on critical issues.

The works of Robert Law (1909), Raymond E. Brown (1982), and Judith M. Lieu (2008) have been seminal. The first offered a comprehensive and challenging reading of First John as *The Tests of Life*, following a threefold presentation of righteousness, love, and belief in the letter.² The second elaborated a historical reconstruction of the theological conflict that led to the Johannine schism evidenced in the letter and provided a thorough reading of the letter through the polemical lens.³ The third parted with the polemical reading—or any hypothetical historical reconstruction—to focus on the assurance provided by the rhetoric of the letter.⁴ All three major paradigms have generated many followers and produced abundant scholarship each. In 2005, Pope Benedict XVI delivered his first encyclical letter, *Deus Caritas Est*, inspired by and grounded in certain verses of First John.

Given this state of affairs, why risk yet another book on First John? What more is there to say?

As I write these lines in late June 2024, each of the past twelve

---

¹ Saint Augustine, *Homilies on the First Epistle of John*, Vol. III/14 of *The Works of Saint Augustine, A Translation for the 21st Century*. Intro., trans. and notes Boniface Ramsey (New City Press, 2008).

² Robert Law, *The Tests of Life: A Study of the First Epistle of St. John* (T&T Clark, 1909).

³ Raymond E. Brown, *The Epistles of John*, Anchor Bible 30 (Doubleday, 1982).

⁴ Judith M. Lieu, *I, II, & III John: A Commentary* (Westminster John Knox Press, 2008).

months has been the hottest in recorded history—at least 1.5 degrees Celsius warmer than the average temperatures before the age of industrialization, when we started burning fossil fuels at an unsustainable rate.[5] In December 2015, the COP21 Paris Agreement identified 1.5 degrees as the limit for temperature increase if we are to keep the planet's ecosystems in relative balance. This was not a fancy goal, but a real geophysical limit to respect, set by worldwide scientific study and insight. Cupidity, comfort, and short sight—if not indifference and mindlessness—are setting us up for failure, with catastrophic consequences. We have set fire to our only home, to our only ride on spaceship Earth, and now we sleep on it!

Not only are we switching off the life-support system that is a stabilized average temperature on the planet, but we are actively eradicating God-created life-forms that will never come back to live with us again. Biodiversity is falling at such a fast pace that we might as well be living through the sixth mass extinction of species on the planet.[6] Our foremothers and forefathers in the faith could never have imagined such a predicament, living as they were in an age of technological humility and abundance

---

[5] United Nations, "Humanity Needs 'Exit Ramp off Road to Climate Hell,' Secretary-General Insists, Urging Bolder, Faster Action to Save Planet, in Address at American Natural History Museum," June 5, 2024, https://press.un.org/.

[6] For a sobering account of the loss of biodiversity and wild habitats within the span of a human lifetime, see David Attenborough, *A Life on Our Planet: My Witness Statement and A Vision for the Future* (Grand Central Publishing, 2020). The well-known naturalist documents a loss of wilderness of 31 percent between 1937 and 2020, with 35 percent of remaining wild habitats at present. This means that one single species (humans) has occupied, tamed, and exploited 65 percent of the living space available on Earth, driving out other species. The United Nations reports one million species are currently at risk of extinction: https://news.un.org/en/story/2024/05/1150056. To review Earth's past mass extinctions and envision the current one, see Peter Brannen, *The Ends of the World: Volcanic Apocalypses, Lethal Oceans, and Our Quest to Understand Earth's Past Mass Extinctions* (Ecco, 2017).

of wilderness. Stories of a flood wiping out entire populations of living beings were set in a mythical past in Genesis 6–9, whereas God's final judgment according to Revelation and other apocalyptic literature adopted the imagery of God unleashing natural forces unto human hubris.

In the biblical mind, life always prevailed; mere mortals could not thwart it. For sacred Scripture to illumine our predicament, we need to learn how to read it with fresh new eyes, from this place and time, from the specific context of the ecological crisis we face. For the past twenty years or so, scholars have pioneered this endeavor,[7] yet no such reading of First John has been attempted so far, to my knowledge.[8]

A "green" reading of First John would be partial and unbalanced if it paid no attention to the plight of the poor on Earth. As theologian Leonardo Boff points out, the most threatened beings in creation are the poor.[9] The ecological crisis hurts first and with mightier brunt the poor, who stand as primary witnesses of the ecological abuse, against us, the rich. We the wealthier can still choose not to see and not to hear precisely because the crisis still barely touches us directly, so efficient is the protective barrier of wealth against it, physically and conceptually. The poor are Earth's children, too—actually, the vast majority of her offspring, the rich among us being the lucky few. Unless

---

[7] For a comprehensive account of biblical scholarship in the age of ecology, see Hilary Marlow and Mark Harris, eds., *The Oxford Handbook of the Bible and Ecology* (Oxford University Press, 2022).

[8] Two books have been published so far on the Gospel of John with the ecological concern in mind: Margaret Daly-Denton, *John: An Earth Bible Commentary—Supposing Him to Be the Gardener* (T&T Clark, 2017); Kathleen P. Rushton, *The Cry of the Earth and the Cry of the Poor: Hearing Justice in John's Gospel* (SCM Press, 2020). In the course of the present book, relevant insight from these publications may inform our reading of First John. Our focus remains on the first Johannine epistle on its own terms.

[9] Leonardo Boff, *Cry of the Earth, Cry of the Poor*, trans. Phillip Berryman (Orbis Books, 1997), 107–14.

we hear the cry of the poor, we are not truly hearing the cry of their mother and our mother, Earth. Time is of the essence. In the end, the crisis will hit us harder too, and by then, it will be too late: the inevitable will be everyone's fate. Hearing the cry of the Earth *in* the cry of the poor now may avert the worst for all. Our green reading of First John cannot and will not lose sight of the poor. Ecology has to become integral, or it will miss its mark and purpose to look after our common home.

In order to honor these priorities, I have no intention of rehearsing the full breadth of scholarship on each chapter and verse of the letter. Scholarly issues and key secondary sources are in footnotes, leaving curious readers to pursue those lines of inquiry on their own. A wealth of insightful publications have fed my understanding of First John over the years, but I do not have the space to pay due tribute and credit to all in every note. I am nonetheless thankful for the contribution of each and humbled by the overall weight of such a debt. Foremost, I openly write on First John as a lay Roman Catholic biblical scholar, in the shining wake of Pope Francis's 2015 encyclical letter *Laudato Si': On Care for Our Common Home*. May his Holiness' teachings endure as I strive to answer his call for an integral ecology from my very limited perspective.

To Hear for Life's Sake

To a large extent, in our days, reading has become a solitary pastime for individuals still valuing the rewards of focusing on more than a few lines of written text. Younger generations in the United States are less inclined to read, and the global pace has sped up so as to considerably limit time for reading in our busy, modern lives. In ancient times, literacy was the privilege of a few, so reading took place quite often in a community setting—out loud, for the benefit of all.

First John was written for public reading in a community of Christian believers, dubbed the Johannine community by modern scholars, after the author of the letter (John the Elder / Apostle / Evangelist[10]), according to Catholic tradition. From the very first verse, we hear an author speak in the first-person plural "we" or "us," addressing an audience in the plural "you." Quite often, the letter invites us to ponder what may happen "if anyone" says something or what might be at stake when "whoever" does or says something. Individual paths are envisioned, but they are discussed in a group setting. You may thus enjoy sharing and discussing this reading with others, since First John was conceived and written for communal deliberation, even as it addresses our innermost beliefs, individual decisions, and personal actions.

In the Roman Catholic liturgy, passages from First John are proclaimed as the Second Reading at Mass during the season of Christmas (from December 27—the Feast of St. John—through the octave of Epiphany) and the season of Easter (once every three years, on cycle B). However, unless a Bible study group is formed for breaking open the word of God, only the hearing takes place, not the sharing. I encourage you to make a move in this direction. We hear God's word not only in silence and prayer but also from others, in the sharing of faith.

All Lives Matter

Humans are social beings. We gather in groups, small to large: family, circles of friends, neighborhoods, villages, cities, and countries. We sort each other by gender, affinity, ethnicity and culture, language, political leanings, religion, profession or line of work. . . . We keep redefining those circles and borders, as

---

[10] Although the author of First John never names himself, tradition has attributed this letter to St. John the Apostle and Evangelist, or to an elder (or presbyter) also named John, since Second John and Third John are letters explicitly authored by an "elder" (2 Jn 1:1; 3 Jn 1:1). For convenience, I use the traditional name John interchangeably with the expression "the author." The purpose of this book does not require an argument on the authorship issue.

we constantly locate individuals we meet or hear about "in" or "out" of said borders. Invariably, we relate better to those we perceive within our group than to those we perceive outside of it. Unfortunately, we also tend to distance ourselves from those perceived outside, and we grow less and less concerned about their challenges and needs, eventually considering them competitors, adversaries, or even enemies. An ill, inbred mistrust of "strangers" prevents us from reaching out in basic human kinship to those we have othered. We no longer hear the cry of the poor among them, only the cry of war and the threat of being harmed or diminished, fueled by our fears.

The Johannine community grew out of the Jewish synagogue in the second half of the first century of our era. Jesus of Nazareth was a Jew, acclaimed as the long-awaited Messiah by some, rejected as an impostor by others. He even lost his life for all that quarreling about him. Those who dared confess him "Christ," "son of God," "savior of the world" (Jn 4:42) were cast out of the synagogue (Jn 9:22; 12:42; 16:2). The outcast formed a community (Gr. *koinōnia*, 1 Jn 1:3) that reached out and embraced "others" like Samaritans (Jn 4:39–40) and Greeks (Jn 12:20–21). First John was even written in Greek. Alas, by the time the letter was penned, a schism had already taken place within the ranks of the Johannine community:[11]

> Children, it is the last hour; and just as you heard that the antichrist was coming, so now many antichrists have appeared. Thus we know this is the last hour. They went out

---

[11] The overwhelming majority of scholars date the three Johannine letters after the Fourth Gospel. So do I. The Gospel reflects the conflict of origin with the synagogue, whereas the letters address internal community conflicts and schism, not even mentioning the Jews. Unless the letters were written at a very early stage before Johannine Christians parted with the synagogue (which seems most unlikely), they reflect a later state of affairs, at the beginning of the second century.

from us, but they were not really of our number; if they had been, they would have remained with us. Their desertion shows that none of them was of our number. But you have the anointing that comes from the holy one, and you all have knowledge. (1 Jn 2:18–20)

Notice the emphatic display of pronouns and how it reconfigures "we" versus "they," reaffirming only "you" as part of "us," no longer "them."[12] Very sadly, notice also the labeling of "them" as "antichrists," that is, demonically opposed to Jesus Christ—something the othered group would have probably denied and resented, if they had received the letter. Because of this sour dispute and break up, we no longer hear their voices: only First John was preserved in the New Testament canon. Some bitterness and blaming pervade the letter, often polemical in tone. We can strive to understand the inner theological conflict that brought about the schism—and we do, in the course of this book—but we need not embrace the rhetoric that condemned other Christians for their misconceptions and shortcomings, even if they became heretics to the main church.

Instead, we can befriend the author of First John for his defense of charity and justice toward the poor, which incidentally may have hardened his judgment on those who left the community. Those who left seem to have not wished to share their livelihood with others:

If someone who has worldly means sees a brother in need and refuses him compassion, how can the love of God remain in him? Children, let us love not in word or speech but in deed and truth. (1 Jn 3:17–18)

---

[12] For an insightful study of pronoun shifts in the letter, see Judith M. Lieu, "Us or You? Persuasion and Identity in 1 John," *Journal of Biblical Literature* 127, no. 4 (2008): 805–19.

> If anyone says, "I love God," but hates his brother, he is a liar; for whoever does not love a brother whom he has seen cannot love God whom he has not seen. This is the commandment we have from him: whoever loves God must also love his brother. (1 Jn 4:20–21)

The author of First John could have extended the same compassion to those who disagreed with him and left the community, but we often fail to see others as "us" when we are hurt by them. All human lives matter, not just those dear to us. We do well to remember this when our reading of First John bids us to consider conflicts of our time, closer to home.

One also can wish that the author of First John had expressed himself in a more inclusive way, explicitly mentioning "sisters," "daughters," and "mothers," who are almost certainly implied but absent from the wording of his text (this is particularly striking in 1 Jn 2:12–14). Again, even sacred authors are conditioned by their times and culture. John is no exception. Patriarchy was prevalent in the Mediterranean culture of the first century, so the author of First John was impervious to the erasing of women from the front scene of social life. They stood hidden behind a crowd of male listeners and actors, yet they believed, confessed, loved, supported the community with their hard work, and shared the word of life, very much as they continue to do today. We are most definitely welcomed and called to read "she" and "her" into the biblical text, as well as to say "her" name out loud in praise of our foremothers in the faith.

All Forms of Life Matter

Creation (*ktisis*) or nature (*physis*) are conspicuously absent from First John. Their absence makes it all the more striking that the letter is so eloquent about life! There is no mention whatsoever of landscapes, rivers, seas, animals, plants, earth, sky, the abyss, or even heaven as the divine realm. The only cosmological term present is cosmos/world (*kosmos*, twenty-three times), yet it is used in a restrained sense, heavily tainted by human sin, as a "world order" or "system" raised in rebellion against God's will. The world remains the object of God's love in Johannine thought (Jn 3:16–17), but it has become alienated from God, under the power of evil:

> We know that we belong to God, and the whole world lies under the power of the evil one. (1 Jn 5:19)

The world has been infected by sin and drifts away from God, obsessed with material ambition, power, and vainglory:

> Do not love the world or the things of the world. If anyone loves the world, the love of the Father is not in him. For all that is in the world, sensual lust, enticement for the eyes, and a pretentious life, is not from the Father, but is from the world. Yet the world and its enticement are passing away. But whoever does the will of God remains forever. (1 Jn 2:15–17)

The world hates the members of the Johannine community ("you" in 1 Jn 3:13), whereas it listens to those who have parted from the fellowship (1 Jn 4:1), because

> They belong to the world; accordingly, their teaching belongs to the world, and the world listens to them. (1 Jn 4:5)

The author of First John reassures his readers that they have not been abandoned in their struggle with the world, for God's presence in them is mightier than the presence of evil in the world (1 Jn 4:4). They are called to resist the lures of the world (1 Jn 2:15–17) and to conquer the world by their faith (1 Jn 5:4–5).

This approach to cosmos/world points to a very negative assessment of what has become of human society, impacting the very world in which we live. One is tempted to draw a parallel with St. Paul's view of creation (*ktisis*) subjected to futility (Rm 8:19–21). The living world needs to join with humanity in praise of salvation:

> In this the love of God was revealed to us: God sent his only Son into the world so that we might have life through him. (1 Jn 4:9)
> Moreover, we have seen and testify that the Father sent his Son as savior of the world. (1 Jn 4:14)

John and his Johannine community share a very narrow worldview, framed by a form of ethical dualism—good versus evil, light versus darkness, God versus world—all playing out exclusively in human relationships, as if only the latter mattered, as if only human lives mattered. Not to consider any of the wonders of creation aside from their subjection to human sin or corruption by human sin—that is, as an evil world order or *kosmos*—is very sad and anthropocentric. On the other hand, Johannine thought does incriminate humanity for its corruption of the created world.

Coupled with a utilitarian view of nature as an infinite quarry for plunder, anthropocentrism has driven so many other God-created forms of life to extinction. We hunt and fish to depletion, we cut down and burn forests, we take over the wilderness and build larger cities and industries—more demanding, more polluting, and always centered on the needs of the wealthier few who possess the most. In this sense, yes, the world runs on enticement, covetousness, and boasting. First John's indictment (1 Jn 2:15–17) stands!

How may we draw from First John a theology of life that is more generous than a message so exclusively focused on human salvation? I am convinced that this more inclusive salvation emerges when we listen to the cry of the poor—when we pay attention to and enact the heart of the letter's call to love each other and share our livelihood with the neediest among us (1 Jn 3:17–18; 4:20–21). The Earth cries with the poor, and John pleads with us to extend compassion. With ecotheologians like Rosemary Radford Ruether, we need to recognize that the same spirit or logic of domination present in sexism (exploitation of women), classism (exploitation of the poor), racism (exploitation of other peoples), and colonialism (exploitation of other peoples' lands) actually runs the indiscriminate exploitation of our planetary resources, ravaging the Earth.[13] All of these sins are connected, as all voices suffering from them are connected, as all of us hearing this indictment are connected in confession, trust, and hope (1 Jn 2:1–2), as we read this book.

Life Together in Gratitude

I started out by stating that First John was all about the word of life. I attempt here a continuous reading of the letter focusing on what insight on life it has to share with readers of the twenty-first century in the midst of an ecological crisis that sacrifices the poor. I will pay heed to the cry of the Earth and the cry of the poor as I read and comment on the letter. For each section, the New American Bible, Revised Edition (NABRE) translation in English is provided upfront, but within the comment, a fresh translation of certain expressions or the layout of the structure of specific verses may help readers see the issues highlighted and discussed. The sections follow my own analysis of the letter, completed as a doctoral dissertation and published in French.[14] For the benefit of English readers, I provide an appendix sum-

---

[13] Rosemary Radford Ruether, *Gaia & God: An Ecofeminist Theology of Earth Healing* (HarperSanFrancisco, 1992), 199–201.

[14] Rodolfo Felices Luna, *Voici le message. La structure littéraire au service de l'annonce dans la Première épître de Jean*, Sciences bibliques 21 (Médiaspaul, 2010).

marizing the findings that underlie those structural choices. All in all, language and rhetoric remain our working tools, but I account for historical assumptions on the original context of the letter.

A word of gratitude is due to the Oblates of Mary Immaculate, whose charism to preach the gospel to the most abandoned has been inspirational to my work and who have generously provided me with the livelihood needed to delve into Scripture. A word of thanks goes also to my peers at Oblate School of Theology, who agreed to this sabbatical time for me to write a book at their expense. Finally, this book would not have seen the light of day had it not been for the trust of my editor at Orbis Books, Rev. Dr. Thomas Hermans-Webster, and that of the Maryknoll Fathers and Brothers. It is an honor to contribute to the Ecology and Justice Series, and to be in such good company. "We are writing this so that our joy may be complete" (1 Jn 1:4).

Rodolfo Felices Luna
San Antonio, Texas

Let Life Bring Joy to All

1 What was from the beginning,
what we have heard,
what we have seen with our eyes,
what we looked upon
and touched with our hands
concerns the Word of life—
2 for the life was made visible;
we have seen it and testify to it
and proclaim to you the eternal life
that was with the Father and was made visible to us—
3 what we have seen and heard
we proclaim now to you,
so that you too may have fellowship with us;
for our fellowship is with the Father
and with his Son, Jesus Christ.
4 We are writing this so that our joy may be complete.

1 Jn 1:1–4

Breaking literary conventions, 1 John opens with poetic and theological conviction. We humans desire life, and Jesus Christ reveals the fullness of life to all the world by incarnating God's all-inclusive love. We have come to experience the good news of Jesus Christ through the witness of others in Christian community—a community of communities, including the author, speakers, and audiences across space and time.

This is certainly not the usual letter heading, as every commentator remarks. There is no indication of who is writing to whom, nor the whereabouts of writer or recipients, never mind the glimpse of a date. First John does not bear the specific marks of a New Testament letter heading, like a blessing or a prayer of thanksgiving for the recipients, which St. Paul has accustomed us to expect. First John's letter heading style only finds a match in the first four verses of the also anonymous Letter to the Hebrews. Both beginnings strike the impression of a prologue to a treatise or a preamble to a homily.

The Train of Thought in 1:1–4

The first four verses of the letter form a well-constructed preamble that grounds both speaker and audience in a relationship that is promised to grow, through a testimony delivered, unpacked, and well received. The author rounds off these verses by encapsulating them within opposite lexical boundaries: "beginning" (*archēs*) in 1:1a and "complete" (*peplērōmenē*) in 1:4. This is the first instance of a technique called *inclusio*, providing a lexical frame that alerts hearers or readers that a portion of discourse or text is to be taken as a unit. This proved very helpful in antiquity, when headings and subheadings, chapters and verses were not available to guide the reception of the text.

Verse 2 clearly stands out as a parenthetical comment on the manifestation of eternal life. Notice how the parenthetical comment is itself bracketed by *inclusio*, as "was made visible" (*ephanerōthē*) is cleverly repeated at the beginning and at the end of the verse (1:2ad). This explains the need in verse 3a to retake the seeing and the hearing that are mentioned in verse 1, completing the thought that is left hanging there before the parenthesis in verse 2. As a result, verses 1 and 3–4 now stand parallel to each other, with verse 2 stuck in the middle.

This is a concentric structure, a style for writing text that might be alien to us but was very much at home in the Bible and the Semitic culture of our ancestors in the faith. Our modern minds are linear and Cartesian, moving from introduction through development toward a conclusion, as from A through B to reach C. Here, though, we have a portion of text built on an A/B/A pattern. This nonlinear writing style accounts for the poetic character of many biblical texts like the Psalms, and it is the reason for the so-called spiral thinking of Johannine literature.[1] The author repeats vocabulary, zooming into a focal point. Here, through attention to proclaiming, the focal point is the manifestation of life.

The insistence on "proclaiming" (twice in three verses) indicates an oral delivery, yet use of the verb "to write" in the last verse leaves no doubt as to the means by which such proclamation may reach its intended audience. The author shifts to the singular "I write" a few times in the course of his message (2:12–14, 21, 26; 5:13), even as he upholds the plural "we" for testimony (4:13–16). The author refers to his writing as a "message" (*angelia*, 1:5; 3:11), which in the original Greek shares the root of the verb "to proclaim" (*apangellomen*, 1:2–3; *anangellomen*, 1:5), as well as that of the noun "angel" (*angelos*,

---

[1] Robert Law, *The Tests of Life: A Study of the First Epistle of St. John* (T&T Clark, 1909), 5: "The word that, to my mind, might best describe St. John's mode of thinking and writing in this Epistle is 'spiral.' The course of thought does not move from point to point in a straight line. It is like a winding staircase—always revolving around the same center, always recurring to the same topics, but at a higher level."

"messenger," absent from the letters but present in the Gospel: Jn 1:51; 5:4; 12:29; 20:12). In fact, "message" (*angelia*) may well be the Johannine version of "gospel" (*euangelion*, i.e., "good message," "good news").[2] If one were allowed to mimic in (bad) English the rhetorical effect of the Greek, one might say he is "proclaiming a proclamation," "messaging a message," or "angel*ing* an angelic utterance."

Setting aside the technical issue of literary form and genre, it is clear that the author wishes to communicate a message to an audience that lives somewhat afar, so the author commits that message to writing and sends it, most probably for oral delivery. In spite of the author's disregard for literary conventions,[3] we may continue to call First John a "letter," but we must accept that we will be left in the dark on much of the circumstantial information that was known and taken for granted by the author and his original readers.

The expectation that the first intended audience would understand without the specifics of a letter underscores the common experience that author and audience had of a shared Christian faith, cast in the peculiar language of the Johannine group, school, or community. Even the otherwise unaware modern reader catches the resemblance to expressions found in the Fourth Gospel and the three letters of 1–2–3 John. These shared expressions invite us to recognize and imitate an insider's way

---

[2] This is convincingly argued by Raymond E. Brown, *The Epistles of John* (Doubleday, 1982), 193, who then moves to translate *angelia* as "gospel." However, First John is clearly not set in the same format as the Fourth Gospel, so it may be prudent for us to keep the distinction by translating *angelia* as "message." Pope John Paul II coined the expression "the Gospel of life" in his 1995 encyclical *Evangelium Vitae*, referring specifically to 1 Jn 1:2 in nos. 29–30, to verse 3 in nos. 80–82, and to verse 4 in nos. 101–2.

[3] To explore the issue of literary genre in more depth, see Rudolf Schnackenburg, *The Johannine Epistles* (Crossroad, 1992), 3–6; Brown, *Epistles*, 86–92; Judith M. Lieu, *I, II, & III John: A Commentary* (Westminster John Knox Press, 2008), 1–6.

of speech. Traditionally, identifying St. John as the author of all Johannine writings readily offered an explanation for this common language: personal style! However, the anonymity of all Johannine writings, the insistent and emphatic use of the plural "we" for solemn witness, as well as an editorial "we" at the very end of the Gospel (21:24–25) support the existence of a network of Christian churches that cherished the heritage of the Beloved Disciple (Jn 13:23; 19:26; 20:2; 21:7, 20), embraced his theological insight, and adopted his symbolical and poetic language. This network of believers has been variously labeled the Johannine community, church, school, or circle.[4] They are the first audience and readers that 1 John addresses. As to the author of the letter, the tradition favors an identification with the author of the Gospel, but this is debated and contested by many modern scholars on various grounds, so the mystery remains.[5] Our reading of First John does not require us to settle the issue of authorship—that is, name an unnamed author[6]—so we refer to him as "the author," "the elder," or simply "John," for convenience's sake.

What is the purpose of this message or proclamation, couched in a letter? We need only scan the text for purpose clauses, which are found in verses 3 and 4, introduced by "so that" (*hina*):

---

[4] The now classic reconstruction of this community of believers and its history is the influential Raymond E. Brown, *The Community of the Beloved Disciple* (Paulist Press, 1979). For a fresh assessment of the evidence see Francis J. Moloney, *Letters to the Johannine Circle: 1–3 John* (Paulist Press, 2020), 1–29. For a skeptical challenge to the theory, see Hugo Méndez, "Did the Johannine Community Exist?" *Journal for the Study of the New Testament* 42, no. 3 (2020): 350–74.

[5] A very comprehensive study of the historical figure of St. John, tracing the development of the tradition and its reception across the centuries, remains that of R. Alan Culpepper, *John, the Son of Zebedee: The Life of a Legend* (Fortress Press, 2000).

[6] Lieu, *I, II, & III John*, 6–9, makes the strongest case to respect the anonymity wished by the author, for his deliberate rhetorical technique to play out the way it was intended to.

- So that you too may have fellowship with us (1:3c).
- So that our joy may be complete (1:4).

First and foremost, the purpose in addressing the audience is to extend and strengthen the fellowship already shared. One presumes at least some degree of fellowship between sender and recipients, in order for them to be acquainted with God as the Father and with Jesus of Nazareth as the Christ, the Son of God (1:3de). The author intends to strengthen those bonds in a common understanding of the faith by developing what that faith specifically entails. At the end of such endeavor, he expects joy to be everyone's holy reward (1:4). True fellowship brings about joy, especially since that fellowship is rich with the divine presence (1:3de). True fellowship spreads out from the circle of intimacy between the Father and the Son, opening wide and welcoming everyone. Who would not enjoy fellowship with God? The author assumes that his audience deeply longs for fellowship with God, so they will then take interest in what he has to say, and joy will abound.

What will prove instrumental in spreading fellowship and joy? Verses 1 and 2 introduce and deploy the topic: life (1:1f, 2a, 2c)!

Life is the object of the verb "to proclaim" in 1:2c. However, the author discloses his topic with poetic strokes, alluding to life mysteriously as "that which was from the beginning" (1:1a),[7] then as it was experienced by the senses one by one (1:1bcde), until it finally comes to expression in a word (1:1f): the word of life. Verse 2 reiterates the manifestation of life, before God

---

[7] Christians familiar with the prologue of the Fourth Gospel cannot miss the connection to, "In the beginning was the Word" of Jn 1:1 and its echo of Gn 1:1. Scholars debate whether John's prologue or First John's preamble came first, whether one is the source of the other, or whether both simply reflect an oral tradition common to both. Our quest here is to interpret First John on its own terms, so useful echoes of other Johannine texts may be noted, but without positing a chronological order or assuming a literary relation that would govern the interpretation.

and then with us. The author presents himself as belonging to a circle of witnesses (1:2b) who testify to the manifestation of life (2cd). Christians who know the gospel may identify this "eternal life that was with the Father" (1:2cd) and that became visible to human witnesses as being Jesus Christ, the Son of the Father come in the flesh, incarnate. Nevertheless, the author does not simply state, "We proclaim Jesus Christ to you." Rather, he purposefully delays mentioning Jesus by name until 1:3e. With this delay, the author can poetically and theologically present Jesus as "eternal life" brought to us. The focus thus remains on life as the object of human aspiration that is fulfilled in the manifestation of Jesus Christ, as he brings God's fellowship to embrace us all, through the mediation of human witness. That is no merely awkward English sentence, moving from object first to subject, verb, and purpose clauses; it's poetic and theological genius.

Life

That life became visible or evident to human witness (1:2ab) may first strike readers as a truism. When was life not an evident phenomenon to all sentient and rational observers?

The adjective "eternal" (*aiōnion*, 1:2c) and the locative phrase "that was with the Father" (1:2d) qualify the specific type of life that has recently been disclosed to human perception. For John, this life is no mere biological phenomenon prevalent on our beautiful planet Earth. It is, rather, the invisible, transcendent, divine power at work, creatively sustaining life on Earth. Life is at work without interfering with physical or biochemical processes at their own level and without having to eventually concede defeat to death, as is the known fate of all living organisms.

From the standpoint of biology, life appears to be a temporary and evolving state of energetic organization of matter. Life seems to move purposely toward self-preservation, self-fulfillment, and procreation, until the complex arrangement dissolves into its primary components and yields its resources to the next generation of living beings. "Ash to ash, dust to dust," we are earthlings, formed from the ground that sustains us, and we shall return to it one way or another (Gn 3:19). Our fate is bound to that of the Earth. We are transient beings, allotted some time to flourish. Our time is precious, because we eventually run out of it. For this reason also, delaying action to help the poor is scandalous, since they of all people cannot afford to wait to prosper.

How might eternal life become a meaningful frame for our living in this precious time? What are we to make of the expression "eternal life" (*zōē aiōnios*), which seems to contradict our most basic experience of what life is on Earth?

If living beings were eternal, the Earth would eventually run out of space and resources for all. Eternal life on Earth would also defeat the purpose of procreation: What would be the use of new generations if the previous ones were still around forever? The very limits of life on Earth are what trigger change and powerfully motivate us to grow into our better selves. Species other than humanity also face challenges, and they adapt and evolve with great effort over time.

In the Fourth Gospel, the Samaritan woman misunderstands Jesus's offer of "living water" and fantasizes about a magical well of sorts, which would always deliver fresh water for her, so that she would no longer have to come out to the village well to fetch water, day after day (Jn 4:10–15). As a matter of fact, had she not made the effort to fetch water on that day, she would not have met Jesus; she would not have felt challenged by this Jew she was reared to hate, nor would she have rediscovered herself as beloved by God in spite of her shortcomings, or become an evangelizer to her entire village. Her effort finally paid off.

In our times, we the rich enjoy the comfort of turning on a tap to have fresh potable water running for us at will. Effortlessly quenching our thirst might have something to do with our mindless lack of compassion for those who do not have such a magical well at their disposal. Just as the Samaritan woman misunderstood living water for easy living, might we be misunderstanding eternal life for easy living beyond the grave?

The expression "eternal life" is first found in the Old Testament in the Book of Daniel, both in its Hebrew original (*ḥayyê 'ôlām*, 12:2) and in the Greek version of the Septuagint (*zōē aiōnios*, 12:2 LXX). For the people of God facing persecution, martyrdom, and having their lives unjustly cut short, Daniel foresees a time of reversed fortunes and justice finally met:

> Many of those who sleep in the dust of the earth shall awake; some to everlasting life; others to reproach and everlasting disgrace. (Dn 12:2)

The basic meaning is living without a time restraint, hence the adjective "everlasting" in the NABRE translation. Here, a sense of elongated, indefinite time is conveyed. The metaphor of sleep is used for death. Some may be said to awaken to live longer, since they did not get a fair chance earlier. The New Testament inherited this hope of salvific reversal on behalf of God's people and saw it fulfilled in the resurrection of the crucified Messiah, Jesus of Nazareth, at the heart of the gospel narrative (1 Cor 15). However, faith in the new life of the risen Christ radically changed the *temporal* perspective.

Since Jesus the Son was raised and exalted to sit or stand at the right hand of the Father in heaven (Lk 24:51; Ac 1:9; 7:56; Jn 20:17; Rev 5), a *spatial* dimension was added: The new extended life was a life by God's side, in God's own dwelling place (Jn 14:1–4), a heavenly life, unbound by earthly constraints. Also, since the risen Christ had received the full measure of God's Spirit, and since he did effectively pour the Spirit upon his church on Earth (Ac 2:33)—empowering us for witness and action—such resurrected life came to be perceived as a powerful one, a life of an altogether different quality than terrestrial and mortal life. It was the very life of God, divine life. Death would not, could not prevail upon it.

This is the possibility of life that lay hidden with God the Father and became manifest in Jesus Christ his Son, according to First John (1 Jn 1:2). It is wonderful news that deserves to be proclaimed so that all may know. The Johannine circle of witnesses, speaking in the first-person-plural "we," is very expressive of their experience of this extraordinary life: they have "heard" with their ears, "seen" with their eyes, and even "touched" this life with their hands. One might think that this simply refers to the first generation of eyewitnesses of Jesus's ministry, him being the divine life made flesh that they could hear, see, and touch. Although rooted in that historical experience, the Johannine circle widens with every generation that joins in the fellowship, hears, sees, and touches on that very powerful life through their testimony—the word of life (1:1f).[8]

The usual translation of *zōē aiōnios* is "eternal life." This tends to evoke in our minds the spatial perspective, as in a life that is otherworldly, the life of God's heavenly realm, impervious to time. Unfortunately, this spatial perspective risks a disconnect with the life that happens in our world within the constraints of time. This disconnect may even prevent some Christians from taking a real interest in the fate of living beings on Earth.

If we only aspire to live by God's side forever in another realm, why care for the fate of this world? Why care for the living conditions of the poor? Why pay attention to the possible extinction of other life-forms?

---

[8] We unpack in the course of this book the various aspects of the topic of life in First John. For an overview on the topic, see Marianne Meye Thompson, "Eternal Life in the Gospel of John," *Ex Auditu* 5 (1989): 35–55; Catrin H. Williams, "Faith, Eternal Life, and the Spirit in the Gospel of John," in *The Oxford Handbook of Johannine Studies*, ed. Judith M. Lieu and Martinus C. de Boer (Oxford University Press, 2018). Full development takes place in Craig R. Koester, *The Word of Life: A Theology of John's Gospel* (Eerdmans, 2008).

Faith in eternal life may end up disengaging us from the created world that God loves, sustains, and saves. To my limited knowledge, no single expression in English properly conveys all three aspects of *zōē aiōnios*: space, time, and quality.[9] Whichever translation is chosen, the idea is to become aware of what one is inevitably missing in every choice, so as not to disregard the other important perspectives.[10] Personally, I have a preference for "enduring life." To me, it renders time and quality (two out of the three aspects); it renders a life that is strong, resilient, and set to endure adversity and remain in some form through time.

How may the three aspects of *zōē aiōnios* resonate with the poor? If the life the author of First John and his peers proclaim were to take place somewhere else (spatial sense), somewhere that the poor cannot or are not allowed to access, this would again remind them of forbidden ground—countries, neighborhoods, clubs, and places of privilege reserved for the wealthy. This would not at all be a gospel message for them. If heaven were a gated community for the successful and the well-to-do, then the poor would be condemned to uproot themselves once again and further migrate, challenging their ban from life as if they had to "storm" their way into heaven, crossing the final border by fooling the surveillance of the cherubim (Gn 3:24).

Thankfully, this is not what the spatial dimension of *zōē aiōnios* calls for or implies. This "other place" life fully happens and is readily available through "hearing" the message, "seeing" it lived out by true witnesses, "touching" the door of their fellowship, and entering into this *relational* realm.[11] Enduring life

---

[9] Mary L. Coloe's "eternity life" strives to convey the quality aspect: "I prefer to translate this expression as "eternity" life to focus on a new quality of life that Jesus is offering, i.e., the life God lives in eternity, which is now accessible in the present." *John 1–10*, Wisdom Commentary 44A (Liturgical Press, 2021), 22n58.

[10] Pope Benedict XVI insightfully addressed the problem of conceiving "eternal life" in his 2007 encyclical *Spe Salvi*, 10–12.

[11] The relational aspect of eternal life in John is highlighted by a number

happens in the safe space of human relations that are lived in communion with the divine presence (1 Jn 1:3de). This is shared space, not exclusive high ground. Consenting to share living space with the poor is quintessential, just as God consented to become our neighbor through the incarnation (1:2).

Time-wise, *zōē aiōnios* cannot be delayed indefinitely if the poor are to enjoy a share in it. The unmet needs of the poor give responding to them a sense of urgency. The perfect tense of the testimonial in 1:1 is thus comforting, since it suggests that enduring life can be experienced now, in the midst of our struggles during our earthly life.

The qualitative dimension joins with the other two aspects in assuring us that enduring life is powerful enough to bend space and time into compliance with God's saving purpose. Enduring life creates the safe space of solidarity in fellowship. Enduring life is strong, remaining when everything else appears to perish all around.

How may the three aspects of *zōē aiōnios* resonate with the Earth? Our planet is the only place available for abundant life to flourish. Other planets might host other life-forms (or not), but there is no planet B for the blossoming of life that has happened under very specific earthly conditions. The spatial dimension of enduring life invites us to consider the entire Earth as sacred space: a tiny blue ball in the vast universe that God has chosen and set apart for life to sprout and multiply, under God's blessing. We stand on hallowed ground; we should remove our pollution like Moses removed his sandals in God's presence (Ex

---

of scholars. Among them, see Thompson, 'Eternal Life," 45: "Thus to have eternal life means to live in relationship to and dependence on the one who gives such life. Eternal life can then nearly be equated with 'knowing God,' where 'knowledge' is understood in terms of personal relationship." See also Jan van der Watt, *Family of the King: Dynamics of Metaphor in the Gospel of John* (Brill, 2000), 201–17; Koester, *Word of Life*, 31–32; Williams, "Faith, Eternal Life," 353.

3:5). Likewise, we should not impede wildlife's flourishing, as we do so by occupying ever more living space on the planet and harvesting resources to exhaustion. Our occupation and exploitation only benefit the financially and materially richest among one single living species. We must learn to decrease our global footprint and occupy less—not more—space.

Time-wise, we cannot delay action or impose it upon future generations. Severe and consistent warnings from the scientific community, committed environmentalists, and the United Nations Environment Programme (UNEP) all point to the same state of emergency for the survival and well-being of the living on Earth.[12] Denial and delay only worsen our common predicament. Life must endure now! By turning our attention to *zōē aiōnios*, our religious discourse can orient our mere biological life to broader and richer notions of endurance, even amid today's urgent crises.

How may we decently claim an enhanced quality of life (third aspect), if human-driven climate change, pollution, and abuse of the carrying capacity of our planet bring biological life down from the lavish diversity of the Holocene geological era? Religious discourse would amount to hypocrisy if believers in eternal life would wage war upon biological life on our planet or dismiss it as irrelevant. God's creation is not irrelevant.

We must realize that we are describing an experience of transcendent reality in symbolic language.[13] To hear, see, and

---

[12] See one such warning issued by the UNEP at https://www.unep.org/resources/global-foresight-report. For more in-depth reading, see James Lovelock, *The Vanishing Face of Gaia: A Final Warning* (Basic, 2009); Jørgen Randers, *2052: A Global Forecast for the Next Forty Years—A Report to the Club of Rome Commemorating the 40th Anniversary of The Limits to Growth* (Chelsea Green, 2012); David Attenborough, *A Life on Our Planet: My Witness Statement and a Vision for the Future* (Grand Central, 2020).

[13] For an in-depth treatment of Johannine symbolism, see Craig R. Koester, *Symbolism in the Fourth Gospel: Meaning, Mystery, Community* (Fortress,

touch the other life that God promises and offers us in Christ is just a manner of speaking. Not even the mystery of biological life is big enough to contain all aspects of God's gracious salvation. Nevertheless, we need some mooring in our reality to conceive and express the divine gift in ways that foster our fruitful relationships. In that sense, the experience of life is so rich that it offers a sure foothold in goodness, serving as a worldly point of reference.

If biological life is indeed our most precious possession on Earth, it can happily provide the language to sketch and evoke what a loving God has in store for us. Given that one is the icon of the other, it is almost tragic to observe that, by pursuing a civilizational curve that eradicates biological life in its full diversity, we are making it even more difficult for anyone to imagine—never mind to believe in—abundant, everlasting, eternal, or enduring life.

Fellowship

The stated purpose of the letter is to extend fellowship to the audience (1:3c). The word for this is *koinōnia*, from the Greek adjective *koinos*, "communal," "common." *Koinōnia* thus means communion, fellowship, a close association for a common and mutually enhancing purpose.[14] In this case, the common quest for the author and his readers is enduring life, such as is found with God the Father and with his Son Jesus Christ (1:3de).

The life that endures is relational: it springs from and is

1995); "What Does It Mean to Be Human? Imagery and the Human Condition in John's Gospel," in *Imagery in the Gospel of John*, ed. Jörg Frey, Jan van der Watt, and Ruben Zimmermann (Mohr Siebeck, 2006); Dorothy A. Lee, *Flesh and Glory: Symbol, Gender, and Theology in the Gospel of John* (Crossroad, 2002).

[14] For a sociological reading of *koinōnia* as ancient Roman *societas*, see Pheme Perkins, "Koinōnia in 1 John 1:3–7: The Social Context of Division in the Johannine Letters," *Catholic Biblical Quarterly* 45 (1983): 631–47.

nurtured by the Father-Son relationship in the Godhead.[15] The author of First John claims to be part of a fellowship of witnesses and participants of such enduring life (1:1–3). This fellowship in particular is more than a club, an association, or a circle of friends with shared interests, since it includes God and the risen Christ (1:3de).

As we will see further along in the letter (3:1–2), fellowship with the Divine can only come from a radical change in human status, from beloved creature to beloved daughters and sons—sisters and brothers of Jesus through divine begetting. One may consider the *koinōnia* that John refers to as the Church,[16] inasmuch as it embodies God's extended family, God's household, the *familia Dei*.[17] To belong to God's household is not merely a social prize to covet; it is the wondrous means graciously made available to us for the divine life to bind us into a wholesome and fulfilling mode of existence.

The wholesome life that divine fellowship provides is said to be found in fellowship with one another, as the community mediates God's and Christ's presence. However, an adversative

---

[15] Feminist scholars like Mary L. Coloe, *John 11–21*, Wisdom Commentary 44B (Liturgical, 2021), 394–98, rightfully insist that we recognize symbolical language here, not to gender the Godhead.

[16] The word "church" (*ekklēsia*) only appears thrice in John's writings: 3 Jn 6, 9, 10. No mention of it is to be found either in the Fourth Gospel or in 1–2 John, although the latter (2 John) is addressed to the "chosen Lady" (*eklektē kyria*) and her children, thereby implying most probably the church. For a presentation of the Johannine church in terms of a new covenant community, see Sherri Brown, *God's Promise: Covenant Relationship in John* (Paulist, 2014), esp. 84–95 on the letters. See also Rekha M. Chennattu, *Johannine Discipleship as a Covenant Relationship* (Hendrickson, 2006), esp. 170–71 and 206.

[17] For First John's use of the family metaphor to designate the Christian community, see Dirk G. van der Merwe, "Eschatology in the First Epistle of John: *Koinōnia* in the *Familia Dei*," *Verbum et Ecclesia* 27 (2006): 1045–76; "Family Metaphorics: A Rhetorical Tool in the Epistle of 1 John," *Acta Patristica et Byzantina* 20 (2009): 89–108; "Domestic Architecture: Culture, Fictive Kinship and Identity in the First Epistle of John," *Acta Patristica et Byzantina* 21 (2010): 207–26.

particle *de* in 1:3d defines the boundaries of said community around the witness of the author and his peers: "with us," "our fellowship," which the readers are invited to join. This implies that other fellowships or communities out there may not mediate the divine presence and the enduring life offered. "We" write to "you," so that "you" become one of "us," unlike others, "they," who do not have a share with the Father and the Son. Although the opening lines of the letter are affirmative, reassuring in tone, inviting, and welcoming, they set the stage and provide the terms for the polemics to follow. At the very least, they indicate that to the fellowship there is an outside world, so that some are not yet "with us," "from us," or simply "us."

Distinctions inevitably draw boundaries, and boundaries exclude others. The poor know this all too well, being always set in a different category: third-class, third-world, wrong neighborhood, wrong set of skills, insufficient funds available, born on the other side of the border. The same logic applies to racism (other skin color), sexism (other gender), and speciesism (other forms of life, never a priority). We have become experts in compartmentalizing beings and detaching and distancing ourselves from others in the very process of othering them. This breaks up the seamless fabric of interconnected lives and runs against the pursuit of fellowship.[18]

The poor belong to our world and belong in God's household. They are not some kind of mistake, failure, or mishap in creation. They are not acceptable losses or expendable beings. According to the United Nations, nearly 50 percent of the world's population—about four billion human beings—live on less than $6.85 a day, with seven hundred million individuals struggling for subsistence at $2.15 a day in 2023.[19] The United Nations

---

[18] Pope Francis powerfully critiques the divisions that impede our perception and exercise of human fraternity in his 2020 encyclical *Fratelli Tutti*.

[19] United Nations, "Ending Poverty," accessed July 18, 2024, https://www.un.org/en/global-issues/ending-poverty#:~:text=Poverty%20facts%20and%20

does not foresee extreme poverty to decrease any lower than six hundred million individuals by 2030, a tragedy that shows how little a priority the poor are in world affairs.

Each one of these lives is precious to God. Each one of these people has a name and a face and a unique personality and should be precious to all of God's children. Those of us who profess the Christian faith may not succumb to despair or helplessness. Rather, we must stand up in solidarity with the poor and unite our voices to theirs in a common plea for compassion, justice, and inclusion.

Many of us living in the comfort of the so-called first world do not realize that we have affordable living at the expense of the poor in other parts of the world. They have little choice but to manufacture goods at unlivable wages, or give away their natural resources, to meet our demand for low prices. Multinational corporations are not the only ones to blame for greed on profit, for they broker cheap labor for us consumers. Such a cruel system works through distancing our neighbors. We do not see up close the people we exploit and the misery they courageously endure; ignorance and facelessness ease our conscience.

Not unlike online bullying, modern slavery thrives on anonymity and distance. More often than not, it is legal, in the sense that the desperate need for trade in poor cities and countries forces governments to settle for unfair terms, including tax cuts, to secure business and employment for their citizens. Corrupt officials take their share in those unfair dealings, while the local population absorbs the cuts in public services, health care, and social protection.

When we benefit from the system in place, can we really say the poor are our fellows? Is any sense of fellowship possible where injustice prevails? Dare we pray to extend a hand of fellowship, while we take to our advantage with the other hand?

---

figures,7.1%20per%20cent%20in%202019.

Fellowship is not just a happy state of mind, religious or not. Simply praying for the poor and sending good wishes will not do (Jas 2:15–17). It requires a commitment to being with others, an acknowledgment of their existence, trials, and aspirations. We have to see and to hear others, to touch their dreams and to let ourselves be touched by their plight (1 Jn 1:1bcde). Fellowship means recognizing what we already have in common (*koinos*), allowing space and time for dialogue, and working out a deeper sharing in word (1:2c, 3b) and deed (3:18), so that our fate is bound to theirs and theirs to ours. This dynamic relationality is *koinōnia* as the Father and the Son wish to establish, strengthen, and extend to others (1:3de).

Furthermore, fellowship is not just a bonus to Christian life. It is an essential part of it. As French Catholic poet Charles Péguy (1873–1914) sharply put it,

> We must arrive together at the good Lord's. We must not go looking for the good Lord the ones without the others. We must all go back together to our father's house. We must also think a little of others. We must work a little for others. What would he say to us if we arrived, if we came back the ones without the others?[20]

At this point, we may wonder what might be the full extension of the term "others." What about other creatures, other species, other living beings? Certainly, the author of First John did not have in mind other creatures, just human beings—and his Johannine readership in particular, to be honest. Yet we read his

---

[20] Charles Péguy, *The Mystery of the Charity of Joan of Arc*, trans. Julian Green (Pantheon, 1950), 39. I am indebted to Fr. Ron Rolheiser, OMI, for bringing up a poignant version of this quote in many of his talks on Christian spirituality: "Where are the others?" Pope Francis also underscores the truth that "no one is saved alone" in his 2020 encyclical *Fratelllli Tutti* (54).

letter today from places John had no idea existed, in a language he never spoke, and with a rich tradition of two millennia of Christian witness he could not imagine. We also inquire upon God's will for our times, and search the Scriptures for guidance amid the global, socioeconomic, and ecological crises we face. Just as the grain of wheat must fall to the ground, break apart, and die in order to yield much fruit (Jn 12:24), so must the Word of God be broken apart as bread to feed the spiritually hungry of our age, lest it remain a Word of God only to past generations. A fuller sense of Scripture is expected when reading today because God does not leave God's church orphaned (Jn 14:18). God's Spirit is sent to teach us and remind us of Jesus's way and introduce us to the fullness of truth (Jn 14:26; 16:12–13), *beyond* but not contrary to what the sacred author intended. In this sense, we must be bold and tread uncharted paths when reading Scripture faithfully.

God also speaks to us through creation (Rm 1:20), and we enjoy a renewed sense of wonder at God's world through the lens of scientific discovery in modern times. The biology of evolution has brought to our attention that similar bodily features are a trace of common ancestry—thus, kinship—between species. We share a striking resemblance to most primates, our closest relatives in the tree of life. They forge and use simple tools, teaching their offspring how to use them too. With due training, apes have even learned to communicate basic thoughts through sign language with us humans, passing that skill on to their offspring. We share with all mammals being born from our mother's womb and being nurtured by her milk during our early stages in life. We share seeing and hearing and touching with so many other animals. We share lungs that breathe air with all that move upon land, fly the skies, and even some that dive in the seas. We share with all vertebrates a column that divides and articulates our body symmetrically. Beyond what our eyes can perceive, we share being made of cells that function much as do all other larger bodies. It even appears that, within our cells, the organelle responsible for generating our energy (mitochondria) shares ancestry and function with the organelle responsible for photosynthesis in plants (chloroplasts),[21] so we may claim distant kinship with all green living things. Last but not least, our digestive system is host to trillions of bacteria (more numerous than our own cell count!), with whom we live in symbiosis. We can thank them for helping us digest our meals, but more to the point: we could not possibly live and prosper without them. "I" am in fact "we," and cannot detach myself completely from other living organisms.

In light of this new knowledge of connectedness that science provides us, how could we restrain fellowship to humans only? Isn't God telling us something important by having made us share so much with all living beings? Would something not be amiss if only humanity showed up to meet with the Creator of all living beings? If humanity is made in God's image (Gn 1:26–27) and shares so much likeness with other creatures, how might these other creatures have a share—incomplete as it might be—in the glory of God's children (Rm 8:19–23)? Entrusted with some form of stewardship over creation (Gn 1:26, 28), are we not called to embrace all of God's garden before we raise it up with us to face our maker?

Enlarging the tent of our fellowship to include other living creatures won't be an easy task. As we already mentioned, fellowship implies seeing, hearing, and caring for others—in this case, animals and plants, tame and wild. That seems like a stretch, given that we already struggle at keeping our families, our parishes, and our communities together. We tend to highlight our differences rather than our *koinōnia* with others. We live under the illusion of autonomy and independence, opposing

---

[21] Joseph E. Armstrong, *How the Earth Turned Green: A Brief 3.8-Billion-Year History of Plants* (University of Chicago Press, 2014), 91–107.

communal interests to our individuality. We alienate human beings based on skin color, place of birth, gender, religion, language, and culture. We wage war among our species and fail to care for our poor. How could we possibly become generous enough to significantly care for other species, beyond our pets?

Such a goal is hard to accomplish, but the way forward is quite simple to conceive. We need to open our eyes to see, open our ears to hear, and stretch out our hands to touch our common (*koinos*) ground, our kinship with all the living. Once we realize how much we belong to each other, depend on each other, how much we are one indivisible web of life[22]—one biosphere "made visible" (*ephanerōthē*, 1 Jn 1:2ad), intricately connected—then we will be less inclined to alienate other living species, hardly any more than we would consent to have a foot or a hand amputated.

To hear the cry of the Earth and the cry of the poor is to pay close attention to the parts of ourselves that we are blind enough to alienate. As we embrace God's calls to fellowship, we must also embrace our magnificent wholesomeness as God's design for flourishing in life together. Much like the Johannine predicament, this is unfinished business, a work of God in progress. Until our "we" encompasses all people and all of creation, our fellowship will fall short of the "fullness of joy" (1:4). [23]

---

[22] Anne Marie Reijnen, "The Web of Life: A Critique of Nature, Wilderness, Gaia, and the 'Common Household,'" *Religions* 15 (2024): 63, https://doi.org/10.3390/rel15010063.

[23] We can only embark on the long journey toward full fellowship with humility and faith in God's promised grace. The steep slope of change required ahead of us may be daunting, but we need not despair. Christian hope is based on God's might and love, not on our strength. Christian hope is not secular hope: it is not grounded on our calculations of what is feasible for us or not, what is likely to succeed or not. As Pope Benedict XVI puts it in *Spe Salvi*, 3 and 31, we need not just a "modest hope" but the "great hope" in God.

Joy

Intimacy with God and with one another brings about joy, abundantly. Christians do not believe in a cruel deity who would have created humanity for toil and hardship, to muse on their tragic fate. Neither do Christians believe in an impersonal or distant God, indifferent to God's creatures. We believe in a God who takes on the role of a parent (1:3d), creating life for life's sake, reaching out through God's Son incarnate (1:2cd, 3e) to give life (3:16), walking with the living (1:7; 2:6), and guiding them with God's light to embrace full communion with Godself (1:5–7). We were made for joy in God's presence. Spreading such good news helps share and increase the joy (1:4).[24]

Yet pain, suffering, and death remain. Some of it is part of the inevitable conditions for life to unfold:

> When a woman is in labor, she is in anguish because her hour has arrived; but when she has given birth to a child, she no longer remembers the pain because of her joy that a child has been born into the world. (Jn 16:21)

Just as all living beings are mortal and bound to die someday, so do we come into the world experiencing some pain and anguish. Giving birth is particularly painful for women, but when the birthing process goes well, there is an end to pain, as it turns into joy when holding their newborn. The evangelist presents joy as the enduring outcome that is worth the temporary effort.[25]

---

[24] Pope Francis set the joyful tone for a renewed evangelization in his 2013 apostolic exhortation *Evangelii Gaudium.*

[25] For an in-depth study of woman-in-labor imagery, see Kathleen P. Rushton, *The Parable of the Woman in Childbirth of John 16:21: A Metaphor for the Death and Glorification of Jesus* (Edwin Mellen, 2011).

Unfortunately, there is much unnecessary suffering in our world, like that produced by lies (1 Jn 2:4), covetousness (2:16), hatred (2:9, 11), refusing to share our livelihood with others (3:17), and murder (3:12, 15). The unnecessary suffering is not part of the fabric of life, but rather life's corruption by human sin (1:7–2:2). In sending Jesus Christ, the Just, God has provided humanity with an opportunity to heal, cleanse, and atone, adjusted to God's purpose, so that the fellowship may be restored and joy may abound.

The joy of the living rises to new heights when it fulfills God's intended purpose for God's creatures. John the Baptizer rejoices that his mission is fulfilled, even as he must fade out on behalf of the Son of God to shine forth (Jn 3:28–30).[26] Having completed the mission for which his Father sent him into the world, Jesus is also exuberant with joy, inviting his disciples to enter it with him, so that theirs may be complete (Jn 15:9–11). Jesus prays that we may completely share his joy (Jn 17:13). We are called to join the fellowship of the Father and the Son (1 Jn 1:3cde). We are called to ask the Father, in the name of the Son, so as to receive the full measure of joy that is our hearts' aspiration (Jn 16:23–24; 1 Jn 1:4).

Proclaiming the gospel is about bringing glad tidings to the poor, so that the outcast and the oppressed may rejoice (Lk 4:18–19; Is 61:1–2). For life to be good to them, too, they need a share in our livelihood (1 Jn 3:17), a part in our fellowship (1:3c), a true recognition in word and deed (3:18) that their lives do count—that they are also beloved children of our Father and God (3:1–2), our brothers and sisters. Unless the poor rejoice

---

[26] There is an important lesson to be learned in the Baptizer's joyful consent to "decrease": it may become the Christian's motto and action plan in the midst of our ecological crisis. See Rodolfo Felices Luna, "John 3:30 as a Spiritual Call for Ecological Witness: A Rhetorical Reading from an Ecocritical Perspective," *Offerings* 16 (2022): 27–46.

with us and among us, our joy may not be complete (1:4). In fact, with the little that they own, the poor are our teachers in the art of joy, for their joy is not dictated or conditioned by our consumerist standards. Their joy is rooted in their sense of community, fellowship, sharing, and belonging together.[27]

Is there a sense in which the Earth may rejoice? The psalmist sings,

> Let the heavens be glad and the earth rejoice;
> let the sea and what fills it resound;
> let the plains be joyful and all that is in them.
> Then let all the trees of the forest rejoice
> before the Lord who comes,
> who comes to govern the earth,
> to govern the world with justice
> and the peoples with faithfulness. (96:11–13)

> Let the sea and what fills it resound,
> the world and those who dwell there.
> Let the rivers clap their hands,
> the mountains shout with them for joy,
> Before the Lord who comes,
> who comes to govern the earth,
> To govern the world with justice
> and the peoples with fairness. (98:7–9)

While these are metaphors, conveying the harmony of creation with God's purpose, significantly all the elements are made to share in human praise of God. Rivers clap their hands, mountains shout for joy, seas resound, and plains and forests rejoice. Notice that the Lord's justice, fairness, and faithfulness

---

[27] This is well noted by Pope Francis in his apostolic exhortation *Evangelii Gaudium* (7).

are the objects of creation's widespread celebrations. Rejoicing takes place when God's ways are honored on Earth, when God's rule is acknowledged. Humanity's ravaging of the Earth is presumptuous and insubordinate to the Creator of all things. If humans dry rivers up, acidify the seas, chop down forests, mine-out mountains, and drain entire plains out of life, nature's voice goes silent. The flourishing of life is what gives God the fullness of praise that is due.

Through our injustice, the poor are diminished, the Earth is diminished, and divine praise is diminished. The abuse of natural resources leaves the poor without a livelihood, and our lack of fairness leaves them without a choice. This is why the cry of the Earth joins with the cry of the poor in one prophetic call for a renewed sense of fellowship and solidarity among the living. The joy of the gospel, the fullness of joy, is at stake (1 Jn 1:4).

2

God's Light upon Us

1:5 Now this is the message that we have heard from him and proclaim to you: God is light, and in him there is no darkness at all.
6 If we say, "We have fellowship with him," while we continue to walk in darkness, we lie and do not act in truth. **7** But if we walk in the light as he is in the light, then we have fellowship with one another, and the blood of his Son Jesus cleanses us from all sin.
8 If we say, "We are without sin," we deceive ourselves, and the truth is not in us. **9** If we acknowledge our sins, he is faithful and just and will forgive our sins and cleanse us from every wrongdoing. **10** If we say, "We have not sinned," we make him a liar, and his word is not in us.

2:1 My children, I am writing this to you so that you may not commit sin. But if anyone does sin, we have an Advocate with the Father, Jesus Christ the

righteous one. **2** He is expiation for our sins, and not for our sins only but for those of the whole world. **3** The way we may be sure that we know him is to keep his commandments. **4** Whoever says, "I know him," but does not keep his commandments is a liar, and the truth is not in him. **5** But whoever keeps his word, the love of God is truly perfected in him.
This is the way we may know that we are in union with him:
6 whoever claims to abide in him ought to live [just] as he lived.

7 Beloved, I am writing no new commandment to you but an old commandment that you had from the beginning. The old commandment is the word that you have heard.

1 Jn 1:5–2:7

First John 1:5 begins the body of the letter by introducing the content of the "message" heard from Jesus,[1] a message, good news, that needs to be restated and proclaimed to broaden fellowship and spread joy:

Now this is the message that we heard from him and proclaim to you: God is light, and in him there is no darkness at all. (1 Jn 1:5)

The good news is that "God is light" (1:5), empowering us to "walk in the light" (1:7). We are not doomed or left to dwell in the dark. This is obviously symbolic language, and we explore it

---

[1] The last person to be named in 1:3e is Jesus Christ, thus becoming the clearest antecedent to the pronoun "him" in 1:5. The author of First John is often ambiguous in the use of pronouns.

in this chapter. Further down the letter, the author recalls Jesus's proclamation in somewhat different terms:

> For this is the message you have heard from the beginning: we should love one another. (1 Jn 3:11)

And he famously adds, "God is love," in 4:8, 16. Noticing the pattern, one can readily see that the core message stemming from Jesus's ministry is recast under two letter headings: "God is light" and "God is love."[2] Each heading calls for a consequent behavior: "walk in the light" and "love one another." Each consequent behavior is modeled after Jesus, who walked among us under God's light (1:7; 2:6)[3] and who laid down his life for us out of love (3:16). By participating in these behaviors, fellowship with God, who is light and love, is secured. Jesus is presented as God's messenger and the believer's role model as son or daughter of God. First John focuses on our relationship with God. It is a theological exposition of what it entails for us to long for communion with God. Jesus Christ is the mediator of such fellowship, and the Spirit of God is the guarantor of the truth of that new relationship, as we show in this chapter (3:24; 4:13; 5:6–8).

The letter can, therefore, be divided into two main parts: 1:5–3:10 and 3:11–5:21. Each main part could be titled theologically (God is light / God is love),[4] or ethically (walk in the

---

[2] Raymond E. Brown, *The Epistles of John* (Doubleday, 1982), 123–29, sees the pattern, which he finds modeled after the Fourth Gospel.

[3] Grammatically, "*he* is in the light" should refer to God in 1:7, since "his Son Jesus" in the same verse clearly points to God. However, "[just] as *he* lived" in 2:6 refers to Jesus's ministry or terrestrial life. Furthermore, the NABRE's "ought to live" and "[just] as *he* lived" in 2:6 actually render the Greek verb "to walk" (*peripateō*), as in "ought to walk" and "[just] as *he* walked." Jesus first walked in God's light, and so we must follow in his wake.

[4] God is also said to be "just" or "righteous" in 1:9 and 2:29. This has led some to argue for a threefold division of the letter, following the three divine attributes. "Light" and "love" are nouns, however, not adjectives. "Justice"

light / love one another). Together, they delineate a way of life that is conducive to the joy of having true fellowship with God and with one another, because such a way of life corresponds with God's holiness and higher calling for us, God's children.

In my analysis, each part is divided into four sections.[5] Each is rounded off by *inclusio*. Here, for instance, 2:7 ends by recalling "the word that you have heard," just as 1:5 had started mentioning "the message that we have heard." Each chapter of this book deals with one section at a time. For each section, as I did for the foreword, I lay out the train of thought and tease out the main topics. Then I explore what those topics may mean to us, who are caught in the midst of an ecological crisis that hits the poor hardest.

The Train of Thought in 1:5–2:7

Introduced in 1:5 as the message heard from the beginning, the main idea is that God is light in an absolute sense: "In him there is no darkness at all." From this general statement, held to

---

is never predicated of God as in the "God is light" or "God is love" formulas. In fact, the text in 1:9 and 2:29 reads, "*He* is just/righteous," and one has to look for the pronoun's antecedent, always hesitating between God and Jesus. While justice is definitely a divine quality, in my opinion it is derivative from God being our light in 1:5–3:10.

[5] The structure of the letter—or absence thereof—is a much-debated issue among scholars. The author's train of thought seems difficult to follow for more than a few verses at a time. Chapters, verses, titles, or subtitles are no sure guides, since the original manuscript had none. My own analysis is based on recurrence of vocabulary, lexical clusters, and semitic parallelism, which may account for repetitions, apparent contradictions, and abrupt topic shifts. My hope is that each presentation of First John's train of thought is clear enough to the general reader and intriguing enough for the scholarly reader to review the arguments and demonstration published in my book, Rodolfo Felices Luna, *Voici le message. La structure littéraire au service de l'annonce dans la première épître de Jean*, Sciences bibliques 21 (Médiaspaul, 2010).

be a foundational truth among readers,[6] a series of dubious claims are considered.[7] These are shown to be wrong and replaced with correct, worthy goals for conduct.

Some may hold that God is light and yet they avoid the light, preferring to walk in the dark (1:6). Claiming to have fellowship with God while walking in darkness is a lie nevertheless—self-deception at best. Others may claim to have no sin at present (1:8) or even not to have sinned at all (1:10), refusing any need for confession or atonement. Some may say that they know God (2:4) or even that they abide in God (2:6) while not obeying God's commandments (2:4). All of these claims are false and incompatible with the belief that God is absolute light.

Conversely, those who walk in the light (1:7), who keep God's commandments (2:3, 5), and who are honest about their shortcomings, confessing their sins, keep the fellowship with one another (1:7b), find forgiveness in Jesus the Just (1:7c; 2:1–2), and taste and know the fullness of God's love for them (2:5).

Toward the end of the section, a rule of life is spelled out: Whoever wishes to be in communion with God must live (or walk)[8] as Jesus did (2:6). To be Christian is to pay heed to Jesus's call to follow him (Jn 8:12), to trust in God's forgiveness, and to walk in life after the example of God's Son. It becomes clear that the message that "God is light" (1 Jn 1:5) constitutes a call to walk in the light, to respond to God's light by obeying God's commandments. This is no recent amendment to the gospel

---

[6] That God is our light and our salvation (Ps 27:1) is a well-established biblical trope (see also Is 60:19–20; Jas 1:17; Rev 21:23).

[7] There is an increased rhetorical intensity in the claims and their refutation, as Duane F. Watson points out in *The Letters of John* (Cambridge University Press, 2024), 31. Here we lack space to examine them in such detail.

[8] "To walk" a certain path is a Semitism for "to live" in a certain way. The Greek text of 2:6 uses the verb "to walk" (*peripateō*), which the NABRE renders "to live." Today people speak about lifestyles. Christians are called to adopt Jesus's lifestyle, so to speak. Still, the image of walking is meaningful and explored more later.

proclaimed by Jesus Christ;[9] it is the "old commandment" that all Christians heard "from the beginning" (2:7).[10]

Theology implies ethics. Communion or fellowship with God is achieved by being attuned to God's holiness and justice, following Jesus's example. Since we are frail and we fail, God has provided a means of atonement in Jesus's self-offering for us.[11] Communion is possible through both an honest effort and a humble confession, not through vain claims of spiritual knowledge, moral perfection, or ritual purity.

Shedding Light on Our Brokenness

The ecological crisis throws in broad relief the broken state of our relations with one another and with the created world. We have an ecological crisis *because* we disregard the poor and the Earth. More often than not, our disregard for the poor and our

---

[9] In the Fourth Gospel, Jesus is the light of the world sent by the Father (Jn 1:9; 3:19a; 8:12a; 9:5). Those who come to him and follow him walk in God's light and become children of the light (Jn 3:21; 8:12b; 12:35ab, 36), while those who cling to their evil ways walk in the dark (Jn 3:19bc–20; 12:35c).

[10] Jesus's teachings are what the first generation of disciples heard "from the beginning" (Jn 15:27). In this sense, the "new commandment" to love one another heard by them (Jn 13:34; 15:12) is welcomed as good "old" tradition by younger generations of Christians.

[11] The wording in 1 Jn 2:2 is difficult to translate. NABRE renders *hilasmos* as "expiation;" the KJV and the ESV have "propitiation"; the NRSV, CSB, and NIV settle for "atoning sacrifice." That the blood of Jesus is involved in forgiveness in 1:7 seems to bear sacrificial overtones. However, in 4:10 it is God who sends us Jesus as *hilasmos* for our sins, out of love for us. Judith M. Lieu does not find any specific ritual reference in the text as to *how* sins are forgiven, so she advises a more general translation as "forgiveness" or "means of forgiveness": *I, II, & III John: A Commentary* (Westminster John Knox Press, 2008), 64–66, 183–84. Jesus's willingness to "lay down" his own life for us (3:16) is how we learn of God's love. We could not love first without that revelation (4:10). Reconciliation with God becomes possible as we learn of God's love through Jesus's self-sacrifice.

kindred creatures on Earth happens when they are treated only as a means to our own satisfaction—not as an end in themselves; a cheap workforce slaves away for us in a quarry of resources—or even as the resources themselves—to exploit to our benefit.

If we dare look away from the distractions constantly hurled at us by various media, sports enterprises, and show business, the state of the world is appalling and worrisome. Certainly beauty remains in any given place to capture our eye, but Earth and the majority of its inhabitants—human and nonhuman—are withering away while we enjoy artificial and fleeting pleasures on small and large screens, in shopping malls, or at arenas. Much of today's entertainment is intentionally designed to numb our senses and to bend our critical minds into compliance with consumerism. The less we think and resist, the easier it is for the few who dominate the market to make their disproportionate profit on the backs of the poor, with our unfortunate help.

First John calls for discernment in our lives. What moves about openly under the sun? What lurks in the dark, counting on going unnoticed—and by whom? God is not made out of photons, but the image that God is "in the light" (1:7a) or even that God *is* light (1:5) serves a purpose. God is about disclosure, integrity, and truth, not concealment or duplicity, manipulation, and lies.

How is it that the true production costs of the goods we purchase remain hidden beneath a price tag? Those numbers and dollar signs do not adequately reflect the unlivable wages imposed upon the poor or the damage inflicted upon the environment, nor do the numbers tell us the depth of those wounds. Economists have come up with a fancy word to dismiss such costs as irrelevant to the equation that yields the price tag: "externalities" or "external costs."[12] Dismissed as externalities, the

---

[12] See Graeme Maxton, *The End of Progress: How Modern Economics Has Failed Us* (Wiley, 2011), 16–17, 193–95.

poor suffer and the Earth suffers for our consumption, without us being aware of our complicity in the matter as long as such externalities are kept in the dark. Those external costs are real all the same. Eventually, the ravages upon Earth build up and appear out in the open, to our astonishment. Eventually, the poor dare to cross borders and show up at our door, demanding justice.

> For there is nothing hidden except to be made visible; nothing is secret except to come to light. (Mk 4:22; Mt 10:26; Lk 12:2)

We may sincerely wish to live our lives under God's light, yet darkness creeps in the back door. We may strive to lead honest lives, keeping away from exploitation and violence, yet we sometimes unwittingly participate in the dynamics of a fallen world. Sin is very much a part of our daily lives, whether we resist temptation or fall prey to it, whether we are conscious of it or not. Who may honestly say, "I have no sin" (1 Jn 1:8), or "I have not sinned" (1:10)? Even heroic, socially committed activists who stand up for the poor, and ecologically sensitive people who give a voice to Earth, are locked with the rest of us in conflict, being part of a world of broken relations in need of forgiveness and healing. As Aleksandr Solzhenitsyn insightfully put it,

> Gradually it was disclosed to me that the line separating good and evil passes not through states, nor between classes, nor between political parties either, but right through every human heart, and through all human hearts. This line shifts. Inside us, it oscillates with the years. Even within hearts overwhelmed by evil, one small bridgehead of good is retained; and even in the best of all hearts, there remains a small corner of evil. . . . If only there were evil people somewhere insidiously committing evil deeds, and

it were necessary only to separate them from the rest of us and destroy them. But the line dividing good and evil cuts through the heart of every human being.[13]

The radical dualism displayed by First John—light versus darkness, truth versus lies, justice versus injustice—is not an ontological dualism[14] that separates people into two camps: the good ones and the evil ones, or the holy ones and the sinners. God's solution lies not in getting rid of certain people labeled as problematic. It is, rather, an ethical dualism of appeal. Choose light, not darkness! Walk in the light, not in the dark! Such decision is for everyone to make, over and again, with inconsistent results, frail and shortsighted as we are.

What is God's way then, according to First John? God's way calls everyone to walk in the light, to discern with the help of God's light, and to ask for forgiveness and cleansing or healing. Without these, neither fellowship nor joy are possible: walking, discerning, forgiving, cleansing, and healing.

Walking under God's Light

Upon listening to the message that God is light, the first step toward enjoying fellowship with God is to step into the light. This obviously means exposing ourselves to God and others for who we are. To live under the light is to dare to be ourselves, not hiding for fear of judgment or criticism. God and Jesus are just (1:9; 2:1). As our light, they reveal our weaknesses, but

---

[13] Aleksandr Solzhenitsyn, *The Gulag Archipelago, 1918–1956: An Experiment in Literary Investigation*, vol. 2 (Harper & Row, 1992), 615. Quoted by George L. Parsenios, *First, Second, and Third John* (Baker, 2014), 75.

[14] For a thorough review of dualism in Johannine thought, see Jörg Frey, "Dualism and the World in the Gospel and Letters of John," in *The Oxford Handbook of Johannine Studies*, ed. Judith M. Lieu and Martinus C. De Boer (Oxford University Press, 2018). Also helpful is John Ashton, "Dualism," in *Understanding the Fourth Gospel* (Clarendon Press, 1993), 205–37.

their justice encompasses mercy. God forgives our trespasses and shortcomings, just as Jesus advocates on our behalf (2:1) and laid down his life for us (2:2). We are seen, acknowledged, forgiven, cleansed, healed, and reaffirmed in our daily quest for the light.[15]

We are also called to see others under God's light. It is easier to judge and condemn others than to exercise the mercy granted us. Practicing compassion requires that we see a fuller picture, not just throw a quick glance of contempt toward the lives and efforts of others—even when we disagree with their choices.

As we look for the fuller picture, we must let ourselves be drawn to inquire about the lives of the poor and the state of the Earth. These are kept hidden—away from the spotlight, in the dark—by the economic interests of the rich and the rhetoric of leisure, easy living, and consumerism. As discussed earlier, four billion people—half the population of the world—live on less than $6.85 a day, according to the United Nations.[16] How do they manage? What changes could help them fare better? Why are they not the heroes of so many blockbuster movies and streaming series? What we do not see neither hurts us nor challenges our lifestyle. Choosing to walk under God's light also means to bring that light upon the lives of the most vulnerable and humbly recognize how our lives are all intertwined.

We grow accustomed to living in—or dreaming about—false environments, disconnected from reality: consider water fountains in Las Vegas in the Mojave Desert (!) or luxury pools in Dubai resorts, while 1.1 billion people live in slums that television doesn't show.[17] We fabricate unsustainable environments

---

[15] We might be tempted to despair of forgiveness in certain tragic or recurring circumstances, yet Pope Francis reminds us that "forgiveness is possible once we discover that goodness is always prior to and more powerful than evil and that the word with which God affirms our life is deeper than our very denial" (*Lumen fidei*, no. 55).

[16] United Nations, "Ending Poverty," accessed August 28, 2024, un.org.

[17] United Nations, Department of Economic and Social Affairs, Statistics

only the fortunate few can afford, while we condemn the many unfortunates to watch these false light shows on screens. What is wrong with this picture? Why should we not grow a spine instead, to resist and denounce the lures of what cannot be equally shared among 8 billion people without desecrating the Earth?

When people become aware of the planetary devastation that we have been ignoring for so long, many end up giving in and getting used to the new normal. We must refuse that new normal at all costs because it is a lie. Nature can and does recover when given a chance.[18] Nothing is normal about bleached coral reefs, contaminated rivers, melting glaciers, or relentless forest fires. An island of plastic junk adrift in the ocean will never be according to God's plan for creation.[19] Even the glimmering Earth, with all its cities alight at night (which could be easily mistaken for a pretty sight), actually tells the sad story of urban sprawl and ever-receding wildlife. With every additional human-made light, God's creatures lose ground and are left with nowhere to hide. Even turning off our own artificial lights is a step toward walking under God's light.

Our ancestors' bodies slowly evolved into an upright position, eventually allowing them to walk on two feet. Humans are a walking species. We can swim, we can dive, we can ride animals, and we can drive or fly engines thanks to our ingenuity and craftsmanship. However, nothing can replace our basic bipedal locomotion, which many of us were once so proud to achieve as a toddler. This distinctive mark of our freedom is

---

Division, "Make Cities and Human Settlements Inclusive, Safe, Resilient and Sustainable," accessed August 28, 2024, unstats.un.org.

[18] See for yourself the astounding revelation of wildlife taking over the abandoned site of Chernobyl—where a nuclear reactor meltdown took place in 1986—in the last scene of David Attenborough's 2020 documentary *A Life on Our Planet*, distributed by Netflix—trailer, story, and link accessed August 30, 2024, worldwildlife.org.

[19] See National Geographic, Education, "Great Pacific Garbage Patch," accessed August 28, 2024, education.nationalgeographic.org.

the means by which we explore our surroundings, interact with the world, and set a course for ourselves. Where and when we decide to go and what path we take or make for ourselves is an expression of our will and priorities in life. This is why the biblical trope of walking to designate our life choices is so meaningful and powerful.

To walk under God's light, like Jesus did (2:6), means to welcome God's light into our lives[20] and to take action accordingly, so that our lives become the true reflection of our desire to know God and to remain in God's fellowship. Action is required, not just words. This is all the more pressing with regard to the poor and the environment. Even if we err, we must take the risk to tread a certain path. God forgives if we lose our way, because only God sees the full picture. No one reached anywhere without first starting to journey. So it is with regard to the poor and the Earth: we must open our eyes to see them under God's light, then take a step forward toward them, following Jesus their Advocate.[21]

---

[20] In his 2013 encyclical *Lumen fidei*, Pope Francis encourages us to see faith both as a foundational "light" to be recovered from the witness of the past, "capable of illuminating *every aspect* of human existence," and as "a light coming from the future and opening before us vast horizons which guide us beyond our isolated selves toward the breath of communion" (no. 4). We welcome God's light into our lives through faith, which mediates it. Yet we are also to welcome God's light coming to us through the faith of others, our brothers and sisters: "Faith teaches us to see that every man represents a blessing for me, that the light of God's face shines on me through the faces of my brothers" (no. 54).

[21] Although the Christological title of Jesus as Advocate serves in 1 Jn 2:1 the primary purpose of reassuring disciples of God's forgiveness, Jesus stands for the community's defender in Jn 14:16. Upon Jesus's departure, God will send "another" advocate to plead on behalf of the outcast, the Spirit of truth (Jn 16:7–13). The poor and the Earth will always have an advocate: the Spirit of Jesus the Just, who sheds light on our brokenness, reassures us of God's forgiveness, and calls us to stand by the poorest on Earth.

3

The Times Are Changing

~

2:8 And yet I do write a new commandment to you, which holds true in him and among you, for the darkness is passing away, and the true light is already shining. **9** Whoever says he is in the light, yet hates his brother, is still in the darkness. **10** Whoever loves his brother remains in the light, and there is nothing in him to cause a fall. **11** Whoever hates his brother is in darkness; he walks in darkness and does not know where he is going because the darkness has blinded his eyes.

12 I am writing to you, children, because your sins have been forgiven for his name's sake.

13 I am writing to you, fathers, because you know him who is from the beginning. I am writing to you, young men, because you have conquered the evil one.

14 I write to you, children, because you know the Father.
I write to you, fathers, because you know him who is from the beginning.

I write to you, young men, because you are strong and the word of God remains in you, and you have conquered the evil one.

15 Do not love the world or the things of the world. If anyone loves the world, the love of the Father is not in him. **16** For all that is in the world, sensual lust, enticement for the eyes, and a pretentious life, is not from the Father but is from the world. **17** Yet the world and its enticement are passing away. But whoever does the will of God remains forever.

1 Jn 2:8–17

God is light, and we must walk in the light to enjoy fellowship with God. Such is the Christian gospel according to First John. The author claims this is the "message," "word," or "commandment" we all heard from the beginning (1:5; 2:7), thus framing the first section of the body of his letter. It is, therefore, surprising to read immediately afterward that—on second thought—the message is actually "new" in 2:8a. The reason provided is that darkness is receding, vanquished by the growing light of truth (2:8c). The new reality shows the truth of the message heard from old. The new context throws light on the initial word spoken by Jesus. The old message is seen now for what it always was: good news! And this message is perceptible in the fellowship of the children of the light ("you" in 2:8b; Jn 12:36) with the Father of all lights (Jas 1:17) and his Son Jesus, the light of the world (Jn 8:12; 9:5).

If reality looks different now, it is because darkness does not completely hold sway anymore: there is light, however little! The good news is that the times are changing. Darkness and light are not in a standoff; the latter is overtaking the former. If the world is latched on to darkness, it will come to pass with the darkness (1 Jn 2:17a). This section is framed by the two references to things "passing away" (*paragetai*), on their way out: darkness (2:8c) and the worldly enticement to darkness (2:17a). In this section, First John calls for discernment of this victory in progress, however slow it may appear at first to be.

The Train of Thought in 2:8–17

The main idea moving through these verses is change. The old commandment to love one another is actually made new in the fellowship enjoyed by the Johannine community. Light is overcoming darkness (2:8c), the members of the community have been forgiven (2:12), they have come to know God's love for them (2:13a, 14a), and they have conquered the evil one (2:13b, 14d). Worldliness is a thing of the past, hopelessly resisting the flooding light of God's will (2:17). The idea of things "passing away" (*paragetai*) is highlighted as the main topic at the beginning (2:8c) and end (2:17a) of the section.

Verses 9–11 associate light with love, and darkness with hate. As mentioned in our previous chapter, Johannine dualism is an ethical dualism. While light and darkness would appear to be cosmic forces locked in battle, in reality, their struggle against each other takes place in the human heart. Everyone would claim to be in the camp of God's light. The criterion to test those claims is how one relates to the brethren:[1] with hate or with love? Only

---

[1] The text uses the masculine singular *adelphos* to designate a member of the Christian community, male or female. In our times, we are much more

when we love do we actually see that we stand firmly under God's light (2:10). When we yield to hate, darkness blinds us to the point that we don't realize where we stand or where we go (2:9, 11). Hate is misleading. Only love illuminates.

Verses 12–14 pause to reassure the readers or hearers of First John of the author's purpose. He is not writing to condemn them but to strengthen their resolve. These verses stand at the center of the section, although they would appear at first to be off topic, a digression.[2] Their repetitive wording shows that they were carefully crafted not only to stand out to readers but to indicate parallelism as the key structural pattern to which we should pay attention.

1 Jn 2:12–13	1 Jn 2:14
12 I am writing to you, children, because your sins have been forgiven for his name's sake. 13 I am writing to you, fathers, because you know him who is from the beginning. I am writing to you, young men, because you have conquered the evil one.	14 I write to you, children, because you know the Father. I write to you, fathers, because you know him who is from the beginning. I write to you, young men, because you are strong and the word of God remains in you, and you have conquered the evil one.

---

sensitive to inclusive language than in first-century patriarchal societies. The Fourth Gospel showcases women as followers of Jesus in dialog with him: the Samaritan woman, sisters Martha and Mary of Bethany, Mary Magdalene— not to mention Jesus's own mother. This precludes imagining that First John would only be addressing men, regardless of the grammatical gender used to designate or address the audience/readership.

[2] Duane F. Watson, *The Letters of John* (Cambridge University Press, 2024), 56–57, still thinks so. He writes, "This section does not seem to fit in its context. It is written in polished parallelism while surrounding verses are regular prose" (57).

Verses 12–13 state three times the author's intention in writing, in the present (continuous) tense: "I am writing" (*graphō*).³ Each statement is addressed to a specific subgroup: "children," "fathers," and "young men." Verse 14 starts all over again, this time in the aorist: "I write" (*egrapsa*),⁴ addressing the same subgroups in that order. While "fathers" receive exactly the same reason for being written to in 2:13 and 2:14, not quite so "children" in 2:12 and 2:14. The reasons for writing to "young men" in 2:14 seem to be an expansion (with added emphasis) of the reasons given in 2:13. The repetitive style may not be to our modern taste, yet the information is not redundant. Rather, it is better nuanced, or at least amplified, the second time around.⁵

Verses 15–16 go back to the alternative between love and hate that we saw in verses 9–11. This time, however, the community of the "forgiven" (2:12b), of the wise who "know" God (2:13, 14), and of the "strong" (2:14) who "have conquered the evil one" (2:13, 14), is summoned *not* to love the world (2:15). The reason provided is that the world is corrupt with

---

³ Strictly speaking, *graphō* is in the present tense, which in Greek conveys a continuous sense.

⁴ In Greek, tenses do not primarily indicate time but aspect. While the present tense shows a continuous action, the aorist (often translated as past tense) envisions it in general or as a point in time. This is why both the NABRE and the NRSV have chosen to render the aorist *egrapsa* of 2:14 as "I write," instead of "I wrote" or "I have written." It is unlikely that First John is referencing another previous writing in 2:14. Tense shift simply adds to the other variations noted in the parallelism of verses 2:12–13 and 2:14. Judith M. Lieu, *I, II, & III John: A Commentary* (Westminster John Knox Press, 2008), 86, mentions that it was common in Greek correspondence to refer to the writing from the perspective of the sender (presently writing) and from the perspective of the recipients reading it (the sender wrote).

⁵ Watson, *Letters*, 57–61, treats these verses as a rhetorical digression, showing the author's use of ancient rhetorical techniques such as *distributio* and *conduplicatio*, which would account for the repetitions.

covetousness[6] and boastfulness[7] (2:16). Coveting is ultimately to hate others for withholding goods from us, or for not being themselves objects, simply at our disposal. Boasting shows how deeply one has fallen into darkness, misplacing the power of life elsewhere than in God alone. To "love" the world in this case would mean to choose darkness, in fact falling prey to hate. Not all that goes by the name of "love" is worthy of praise. God's light is necessary to discern true love from mere lust, desire, or coveting. Because of the fallen state of the world, worldliness and worldly standards are never a sure guide.

Verse 17a associates the world with the darkness that is "passing away," recalling the main topic introduced in verse 8c. Since verses 15–16 pick up the love/hate alternative of verses 9–11, they run parallel to each other, with verses 12–14 standing in between, at the center of the section.[8] The faithful remain rooted in the light of God's will (2:12–14, 17b), while the world of covetousness and boasting fades out into darkness (2:8c, 17a).

---

[6] The same Greek word *epithymia* lies behind the NABRE's "sensual *lust*" and "*enticement* for the eyes" in 2:16. The NRSV sticks to the same word "*desire*" in both instances: "*desire* of the flesh" and "*desire* of the eyes," which is a more literal translation. In my view, the sexual overtones of "sensual lust" are misleading. The triadic sequence of "*epithymia* of the flesh" and "*epithymia* of the eyes" culminates in "a pretentious life," which actually points to a materialistic lifestyle. This may comprise but not necessarily be restricted to satisfying immoderate sexual cravings. Covetousness seems the overarching concept driving the triad in 2:16.

[7] The Greek expression is *alazoneia tou biou*, rendered by the NABRE as "a pretentious life" and by the NRSV as "the pride in riches." I would forward the following translation: "boasting of a livelihood," to underscore the corruption of the means to support terrestrial life. *Livelihood* should serve to spread *life*, not grow as an end in itself.

[8] Although Watson, *Letters*, 57, notices the topic of love in the preceding and following verses, he fails to see the concentric structure that ensues. Granted, vocabulary may not be as well-knit as in 2:12–14, yet a clear pattern is discernible: A. passing away (2:8); B. love/hate (2:9–11); C. I am writing (2:12–13); C′. I write (2:14); B′. love/not love (2:15–16); A′. passing away (2:17).

Do Not Love the World?

In Johannine thought, the "world" is very much loved and cared for by its creator:

> For God so loved the world that he gave his only Son, so that everyone who believes in him might not perish but might have eternal life. For God did not send his Son into the world to condemn the world, but that the world might be saved through him. (Jn 3:16–17)

First John echoes this faith twice in the letter, later on:

> In this way the love of God was revealed to us: God sent his only Son into the world so that we might have life through him. (1 Jn 4:9)
>
> Moreover, we have seen and testify that the Father has sent his Son as savior of the world. (1 Jn 4:14)

Of Jesus, it has already been said so far that

> He is expiation for our sins, and not for our sins only, but for those of the whole world. (1 Jn 2:2)

So, how can the author of First John suddenly advise his readers in 2:15 *not* to love the world or anything that is in the world? This prohibition is so bold that it requires qualification. The author offers an explanation immediately afterward:

> For all that is in the world—flesh that covets, eyes that covet, and the boasting of a livelihood—is not from the Father but is from the world. (1 Jn 2:16, translation mine)

First John delivers a very pessimistic assessment of the way the "world" conducts its affairs, in isolation from and in opposition to God. The statement is too reductive, we might think, as there are good people in the world who love and graciously help others, instead of coveting and boasting of riches. Who could say otherwise? The author's statement might actually be read as an indictment against himself and his community, who still live in the world and are part of the world. But are they really?

As in many other Johannine verses, the "world" is taken here not as the place where people live, humanity, or God's creation, but as the *organized resistance to God's will* that seems to rule and dominate human relations overall. The world that is under scrutiny is the world as a *system in power*.[9] There are powers on Earth that actively resist God's will, which is why the world in its current state does not look like the kingdom of God, and why we Christians pray, "thy Kingdom *come*, on Earth *as* it is in heaven." These powers dominate over those who long to see durable change for good in the world. Toward the end of the letter, the author reminds his readers,

> We know that we belong to God, and the whole world is under the power of the evil one. (5:19)

The revelation of God's will that Jesus and his disciples spread runs against the vested interests of the powerful on Earth, who prefer to cling to their privilege rather than yield to God's authority and compassion for the poor. In doing so, worldly powers coalesce and organize their mundane resistance to God's light, choosing to remain in the dark:

---

[9] Margaret Daly-Denton also defines the Johannine "world" (*kosmos*) as "that system of values and practices that is antithetical to 'the way' of Jesus." *John: An Earth Bible Commentary. Supposing Him to Be the Gardener* (T&T Clark, 2017), 193.

> And this is the verdict, that the light came into the world, but people preferred darkness to light, because their works were evil. For everyone who does wicked things hates the light and does not come toward the light, so that his works might not be exposed. (Jn 3:19–20)

In First John, "evil works" and "wicked things" are "flesh that covets, eyes that covet, and the boasting of a livelihood" (1 Jn 2:16, translation mine). These values seem to run the world, and many people are deceived into believing that these values could bring about the fullness of joy.

Being a minority that is alienated from the values of the majority, the Johannine community perceived itself as not belonging to the world any more than Jesus did. They were the misfits. In his closing prayer in John's Gospel, Jesus says,

> I gave them your word, and the world hated them, because they do not belong to the world any more than I belong to the world. I do not ask that you take them out of the world but that you keep them from the evil one. They do not belong to the world any more than I belong to the world. (Jn 17:14–16)

Just as Jesus the savior went unrecognized or even rejected by the world he was sent to save, so do the disciples who speak in his name and walk in his wake in the Gospel (Jn 1:10–11):

> If the world hates you, realize that it hated me first. (Jn 15:18)
>
> Do not be amazed, then, brothers, if the world hates you. (1 Jn 3:13)

Their misrecognition and rejection are precisely why the author of First John's proclamation of the message and spreading of the fellowship evermore (1:1–4) is of the utmost importance. The author must awaken God's children to the lies of the world, pulling them out of the sphere of influence of the covetous, the powerful, and the boastful, so that darkness recedes and God's light takes over. God's children are called to love others—and also to see worldly values for what they are and not to embrace them uncritically.

A World on the Brink of Collapse

"The world and its enticement are passing away," we read in 1 Jn 2:17a. This was written with the conviction that only God's plans, God's will, and God's work remain forever (2:17b). The rest is inconsistent and transient at best, a temporary arrangement that provides no security in the long run. First John shares with St. Paul an apocalyptic outlook on reality:

> I tell you, brothers, the time is running out. From now on, let those having wives act as not having them, those weeping as not weeping, those rejoicing as not rejoicing, those buying as not owning, those using the world as not using it fully. For the world in its present form is passing away. (1 Cor 7:29–31)

The original thrust of Christian faith—"what we heard from the beginning"—flowed from the paschal mystery: the resurrection of Christ ushered a new era of peace, in which God would finally establish God's rule over the world, providing justice, healing, and a hopeful future for the poor. The way things are run in the world is bound for change!

The apocalyptic outlook of the Christian faith is about the long-awaited reversal of the world order by God, not about the destruction of creation. Paul also insists on how creation awaits its liberation:

> For creation awaits with eager expectation the revelation of the children of God; for creation was made subject to futility, not of its own accord but because of the one who subjected it, in hope that creation itself would be set free from slavery to corruption and share in the glorious freedom of the children of God. We know that all creation is groaning in labor pains even until now. (Rom 8:19–22)[10]

The image of "labor pains" is strongly suggestive of new life coming forth. A new era, not total annihilation, lies ahead of us. Nonetheless, for that new era of life to be ushered in, the old scheme of things must be let discarded. The old ways and the new ways cannot coexist. There is no darkness in God (1:5); if God's light takes over (2:8d), then the darkness that prevailed in the world and that presented itself as false enlightenment—the covetousness of eyes and flesh, and the boasting of a livelihood—must pass away for good (2:8c, 16, 17a).

The old system of exploitation in power is to be toppled—or will collapse of its own weight, like a statue of gold, silver, and bronze standing over feet of iron mixed with clay (Dn 2:31–35). No more draining the Earth of its resources for consumerist and hoarding purposes, customizing extra commodities for the richest in the world. No more building empires upon the backs of the poor and then excluding them from the party. A much simpler lifestyle is called for; most of us would benefit from learning to have humbler standards and expectations in life.[11] This is good news for the Earth and for the poor. Whether it

---

[10] This Pauline text is a go-to text in ecotheology, even though exegesis of it raises many questions. See David G. Horrell, Cherryl Hunt, and Christopher Southgate, *Greening Paul: Rereading the Apostle in a Time of Ecological Crisis* (Baylor University Press, 2010).

[11] See the groundbreaking 1973 book by Ernst Friedrich Schumacher, *Small Is Beautiful: Economics as If People Mattered* (Harper Perennial, 2014).

also becomes good news for us is up to us. But it is happening, whether we like it or not.

For the past fifty years or so, economists and scientists have analyzed and projected the curve of current trends in development.[12] Many serious scholars share the conclusion that humanity is mindlessly rushing to global collapse.[13] This is not doomsday cheap talk but science supported by data and sound theoretical models. The only immediate senses of this rush we might experience in our limited daily lives are city traffic jams, overcrowded lodging, price hikes, and certain commodities that are occasionally out of stock. We don't get to see that greater worldwide demand for every form of produce or product available under the sun—for manufactured goods, technology, energy, transportation, and other services—is draining the Earth of its resources beyond its carrying capacity, let alone its natural capacity to regenerate.

Not everything is or can be recycled. Nurtured by the merchant world, we live under the illusion that unlimited riches are available for extraction, processing, and purchase by every generation *forever*. Yes, the Earth is a big planet for an individual, but it is not big enough if eight billion people strive to live by the same standards as the "successful" few who boast of their lifestyles in various media. We forget that our planet is a sphere: space and goods are limited to what can be found within that sphere. What will we do when the last drop of fossil

---

[12] The classic 1972 study presented to the Club of Rome is by Donella Meadows, Dennis Meadows, Jørgen Randers, and William Behrens III, *The Limits to Growth: A Report for the Club of Rome's Project on the Predicament of Mankind* (Universe, 1972). After collecting data for thirty years, the authors produced an update that corroborated predictions: *The Limits to Growth. The 30-Year Update* (Chelsea Green, 2004).

[13] See Jørgen Randers, *2052: A Global Forecast for the Next Forty Years—A Report to the Club of Rome Commemorating the 40th Anniversary of The Limits to Growth* (Chelsea Green, 2012). See also Pablo Servigne and Raphaël Stevens, *How Everything Can Collapse: A Manual for Our Times* (Polity, 2020), trans. Andrew Brown from the 2015 original in French.

fuel is pumped out of the Earth's crust? Or when all the copper is used up by construction of electrical networks, when no more lithium is left to power up batteries?[14] And so on . . .

Before we reach those dry points on each resource, they will become more difficult to extract, and demand will drive prices to a prohibitive level for most of the Earth's population. When we stop to consider that half of humanity must live on less than seven dollars a day, we realize that half of humanity is already under strenuous conditions that everyone would like to avoid and the fortunate would rather not consider. Today's poor already face the consequences of our immoderate, boastful lifestyle. The next generations will face an unfair, dire future, unless we renounce the enticement of consumerism.

This is not simply the result of overpopulation. Yes, we have seen a tremendous growth in human population in the past two centuries, going from one billion in 1800 to eight billion in 2022.[15] However, the strain on planetary resources comes from the wealthy minority, not the overwhelming majority.[16] It is not the absolute number of living people that is pushing the world to the tipping point of collapse. It is, rather, the lifestyles of the fortunate and powerful. Eight billion people cannot live in an uptown gated community, wear Prada, drive a sports car, eat a beefsteak for dinner, and post their happiness on social media with their own iPhone. Eight billion people cannot fly to and tour the cities of the world or go on expensive cruises to exotic islands. This would take up the resources of many planets.[17] We

---

[14] UN Environment Programme, "We're Gobbling Up the Earth's Resources at an Unsustainable Rate," April 3, 2019, unep.org.

[15] UN Population Fund, World Population Trends, accessed September 7, 2024, unfpa.org.

[16] See Cody Peluso's analysis, "Earth Overshoot Day: The Bitter Truth of Overconsumption in the Global North," Population Media Center, August 1, 2023, populationmedia.org.

[17] In 2024, the Earth Overshoot Day was calculated to be August 1. This is "the date when humanity's demand on nature's resources surpasses Earth's capacity to regenerate them for the given year." See The Club of Rome, "Earth Overshoot Day 2024 Falls on August 1st," July 30, 2024, clubofrome.org.

have to learn to scale our lifestyles down to a sustainable level.[18] We must ask ourselves, *If I did this, if I purchased this, could eight billion people do it, too, without the planet running out of it?*

Whatever we choose to do, the economic *system* of world exploitation is bankrupt and doomed to "pass away" (1 Jn 2:8c, 17a) because it is simply not sustainable.[19] Sadly, the more we delay our ecological conversion, the more the poor suffer and the less planet there is left for other living species and future generations.[20]

To Set Our Hope in the Light

The development just described may be cause for concern and action but should not lead to despair. Even when First John saw the scheme of this world of covetousness passing away (2:17a), he also saw the true light already shining (2:8d) and those who strive to do God's will remaining for the world to come (2:17b).

Our hope lies with the poor, our masters in simplicity who, by their very lives, prophesy the coming of a new world—and by their example, testify that it is possible to live with less than what seems indispensable to us. If their struggles, their pain, and their grief are our indictment, their sense of *fellowship* is

---

From August through December, we live on goods stolen from our children and grandchildren. The ecological footprint is heaviest on the rich countries of the global north, with the United States requiring five planets to account for its consumption of resources. Of course, not everyone in the United States adds equally to that national footprint.

[18] Pope Francis reminds us that "Christian Spirituality proposes an alternative understanding of the quality of life, and encourages a prophetic and contemplative lifestyle, one capable of deep enjoyment free of the obsession with consumption. We need to take up an ancient lesson, found in different religious traditions and also in the Bible. It is the conviction that 'less is more.'" *Laudato Si'*, no. 222.

[19] For sustainable goals, see UN Environment Programme, "UNEP and the Sustainable Development Goals," accessed September 7, 2024, unep.org/. Learn also about the *Laudato Si'* goals and take action through the Laudato Si' Action Platform: https://laudatosiactionplatform.org/.

[20] On ecological conversion, see Pope Francis, *Laudato Si'*, nos. 216–21.

a promise, and the *joys* they share are also our hope. Theirs is the *light*, and the risen Jesus *walks with* them, if we care to join.

Our hope lies with the Earth, which has survived five mass extinction events in the 3.5-billion-year history of life it has graciously harbored. Through ice ages and volcanic ages, through the reshaping of continents and bodies of water, the Earth has endured. Billions of life-forms have evolved on it and become ever richer and more complex. We can set our trust upon the wisdom of our host, even as we must care for it and not take our environmental conditions for granted.[21]

Our hope lies with God,[22] creator of heaven and Earth, who, by God's gracious will, sustains and endears every single created life-form. When we are tempted to despair for the poor or for the future of life on Earth, may God's light shine upon us, guiding our very next step forward.[23]

---

[21] James Lovelock's Gaia theory sees the planet as a self-adjusting living organism: one complex ecosystem that has survived five mass extinctions under extreme weather conditions. The question is not whether life will survive human hubris on Earth. Life will prevail; the question is whether humanity will relieve Gaia of the pressure exerted upon it, or succumb to Gaia's adjustment of temperature and other environmental factors to favor other species living on it. An extremely hot climate is unwelcoming to humans, but other life-forms may thrive on it. See James Lovelock, *Gaia: A New Look at Life on Earth* (Oxford University Press, 1979); *The Ages of Gaia* (Oxford University Press, 1988); *The Revenge of Gaia: Earth's Climate in Crisis and the Fate of Humanity* (New York: Basic, 2006); *The Vanishing Face of Gaia: A Final Warning* (Basic, 2009).

[22] Pope Francis has disentangled Christian hope from secular positive thinking or "hopeful" expectations in a series of profound reflections delivered in general audiences held in Rome from December 2016 through March 2017: *On Hope* (Loyola, 2017). See also the bull of indiction of the year 2025 Jubilee on hope, *Spes non confundit*.

[23] To help ordinary people take their first steps toward lowering their footprint and contributing to sustainable development, the United Nations has published *The Lazy Person's Guide to Saving the World*, un.org. For policy changes needed in our societies—policies we can vote for and demand of our government representatives in a democracy—see, in more depth, Graeme Maxton and Jørgen Randers, *Reinventing Prosperity: Managing Economic Growth to Reduce Unemployment, Inequality, and Climate Change—A Report to the Club of Rome* (Greystone, 2016).

4

Remaining True

2:18 Children, it is the last hour; and just as you heard that the antichrist was coming, so now many antichrists have appeared. Thus we know this is the last hour.

19 They went out from us, but they were not really of our number; if they had been, they would have remained with us. Their desertion shows that none of them was of our number. **20** But you have the anointing that comes from the holy one, and you all have knowledge. **21** I write to you not because you do not know the truth but because you do, and because every lie is alien to the truth. **22** Who is the liar? Whoever denies that Jesus is the Christ. Whoever denies the Father and the Son, this is the antichrist. **23** No one who denies the Son has the Father, but whoever confesses the Son has the Father as well.
24 Let what you heard from the beginning remain in you. If what you heard from the beginning remains in you, then you will remain in the Son and in the

Father. **25** And this is the promise that he made us: eternal life. **26** I write you these things about those who would deceive you. **27** As for you, the anointing that you received from him remains in you, so that you do not need anyone to teach you. But his anointing teaches you about everything and is true and not false; just as it taught you, remain in him.

28 And now, children, remain in him, so that when he appears we may have confidence and not be put to shame by him at his coming.

1 Jn 2:18–28

Not only are the times changing, the Johannine author and his community are facing critical times. Many have forsaken the fellowship, leaving their former brothers and sisters in dismay. A theological dispute appears to have fueled dissent and discomfort to the point that prayer in common was no longer an option. Those who left the fold continue their life of faith on their own, and they teach their ways to others, while those who remain behind are left hurting, with so many questions: Did they make the right choice? Who has the right version of the gospel? How could anyone tell truth from falsehood? The author of the letter sees the urgency to address the trauma of schism upfront, without delay or compromise in mind.

The section is encapsulated by references to the present context ("so now," 2:18c; "and now," 2:28a), interpreted in light of Christian expectations of the ultimate struggle between good and evil in the end times ("last hour," 2:18ad; "the antichrist was coming," 2:18b; "when he appears," 2:28b; "at his coming," 2:28c).[1] The author intends to reassure his flock that they have

---

[1] Judith M. Lieu, *I, II, & III John: A Commentary* (Westminster John Knox Press, 2008), 114, notices the recurring vocabulary and keeps 2:18–28

made the right choice and encourages them to remain steadfast in that choice (2:27d, 28a).

The Train of Thought in 2:18–28

Verses 2:18–19 recall the painful experience of a significant loss of community members. Their "going out" (2:19a) is equated with the "appearance" of many antichrists (2:18c). First John denies them any former part in the community: they were not really true members, or else they would have remained (2:19). Their true option becomes manifest, that's all, which means their claim to bear the Christian name was false and misleading to others. Such a showdown was in fact to be expected in the end times, before the Parousia, or second coming, of Christ.[2] By reframing the schism as a "last hour" crisis—the moment of truth—First John provides a way for the remnants of his community to process the loss and to strengthen their resolve to remain.[3]

---

together. A number of commentaries miss that observation, giving priority to the new address "And now, children" as the start of a new section from 2:28 onward. See, for instance, John Painter, *1, 2, and 3 John*, Sacra Pagina 18 (Liturgical, 2002), 214; George L. Parsenios, *First, Second, and Third John* (Baker, 2014), 91; Duane F. Watson, *The Letters of John* (Cambridge University Press, 2024), 80.

[2] See, for instance, outside of the Johannine corpus, Mk 13:19–23; 2 Th 2:1–12; 2 Tm 3:1–9; 2 Pt 2:1–17. However, only here in 1 Jn 2:18; 4:3, and in 2 Jn 7, does the word "antichrist" (*antichristos*) appear in the New Testament. Mk 13:22 has *pseudochristoi*, which both the NABRE and the NRSV translate as "false messiahs."

[3] As mentioned in this book's foreword, these verses have provided a window into the historical context of First John. Following Raymond E. Brown's masterly commentary, *The Epistles of John,* Anchor Bible 30 (Doubleday, 1982), many scholars have interpreted the letter as a pastoral response to the schism. Such reading has been labeled "polemical" by those who, following Lieu, *I, II, & III John*, do not see the issue as pervasive in the letter. Painter offers a nuanced critique of the so-called nonpolemical interpretation in *1, 2, and 3 John*, 84–93. In recent times, the very existence of a Johannine community

Verses 2:20–21 and 2:26–27 run parallel to each other.[4] In both units, the author appeals to the "anointing" received as the means to discern true from false Christianity. "Christ" means "Anointed," so Christians are the anointed followers of Christ, consecrated to further Christ's work in the world. When in doubt about the faith, First John recommends going back to basics: What were we anointed for? What was Christ anointed for? Any further doctrinal development cannot possibly contradict the initial thrust of the good news, the message heard from the beginning. Any person who knows what he or she was anointed for can run religious claims by the test of their calling to follow Christ. Any Christian is empowered to discern the true path that Jesus trod. In this sense, Christians need no other master than Christ. Whenever they are taught in the faith, Christians can and must run all teachings by the test of their anointing. First John's brotherhood and sisterhood are encouraged to discern accordingly, not to be dazzled by novelties or feel diminished by those boastful teachers who would prey on their feeling ignorant.

Verses 2:22–23 and 2:24–25 stand parallel to each other at the center of this section. No one has direct access to God the Father aside from God's Son, Jesus the Christ, the Anointed One. Any Christian theology that only pays lip service to Jesus, while making bold claims about God unrelated to the mystery of God revealed *in* Jesus, is a misrepresentation of true Christianity.

---

has come under close scrutiny. Hugo Méndez and Elizabeth J. B. Corsar, for instance, read 1–3 John as pseudohistorical or as epistolary fiction in Christopher Seglenieks and Christopher W. Skinner, eds., *The Johannine Community in Contemporary Debate* (Lexington / Fortress Academic, 2024), 139–71. I deem the pastoral paradigm still more compelling than its critiques, which is why this book assumes the trauma of schism as a reading lens for First John.

[4] Focusing on the rhetorical argument, Watson, *The Letters of John,* 67, sees this section structured by "three negative characterizations of the secessionists and their message (vv. 18–19, 22–23, 26), juxtaposed with three positive affirmations of the faithful and their spiritual status (vv. 20–21, 24–25, 27)."

The very intimate communion between the Father and the Son is what beckons all Christians into a share in eternal life (2:25). First John reminds his shaken community of this Christological truth at the heart of their faith. Any playing down of Jesus for whatever reasons flags such teaching as anti-Christian, a lie flowing from an antichrist movement, such as the one that drained their ranks.

Verse 2:28 brings this difficult section to a comforting closure, recalling the theme of the last hour that started in 2:18 but putting forward Christ's return, which will thwart the antichrist schemes and reaffirm those rooted in their calling, in their anointing.

The Last Hour

When Jesus starts his ministry, Mark summarizes the good news he preached in the following terms:

This is the time of fulfillment. The kingdom of God is at hand. Repent, and believe in the gospel. (Mk 1:15)
The time is fulfilled, and the kingdom of God has come near; repent, and believe in the good news. (Mk 1:15, NRSV)

In both translations, the sense is that God's plan is in motion, reaching its completion stage as Jesus speaks. The announcement that God is about to take over and establish God's rule on Earth is the good news to spread and to believe. A change in our lives is called for, one that acknowledges God's sovereign rule over us and God's agenda over our selfish or mundane inclinations. To capture more vividly the thrust of Jesus's calling, we could paraphrase Mark 1:15 thus:

Time's up! God is now in command. Fall in line with God's priorities, and trust in the goodness of this happy turn of events.

The arrest, trial, and execution of Jesus of Nazareth threw his followers into disarray. Yet the resurrection of Christ reignited the hope and emboldened them to proclaim the good news themselves. Ever since, setbacks are reinterpreted as turning points, anticipating God's final victory, when Christ will appear in glory.

Paul the apostle qualifies Christian existence as marked by the resurrection of Christ—in a sense, engulfed by it, absorbed by Christ's victory over death, receiving divine adoption, empowered and led by the Spirit, dedicated to serve in the kingdom of God (Rm 6–8). Caught within that movement, the baptized in Christ participate in the fulfillment of the times: "Us, upon whom the end of the ages has come" (1 Cor 10:11).

In light of this, the Christian way of life is marked by awareness of our times. We must be attentive to the "signs of the times" (Mt 16:3).[5] Christians cannot disengage from the challenges of life on Earth but are called to join in "the joys and the hopes, the griefs and the anxieties of men of this age, especially those who are poor or in any way afflicted."[6] In every circumstance and at every turn of the ages, Christians are called to read the signs of the times and attend to "the last hour" (1 Jn 2:18ad) that is manifest.

In the present day, the environmental crisis is the major sign of our times. It is not only a calamity in itself, with soaring temperatures and all the disturbances that ensue, affecting all ecosystems and life-forms on Earth. This crisis is also a sign of human greed and hubris, disregarding our impact on creation. It is a sign of how humans for millennia have been treating our

---

[5] See the use of the biblical expression in the apostolic constitution *Humanae salutis*, no. 4, whereby Pope St. John XXIII called the Second Vatican Council in 1961.

[6] See the opening lines of the apostolic constitution *Gaudium et spes*, no. 1, elaborated by the fathers of the Second Vatican Council and promulgated by Pope Paul VI in 1965.

own poor, now bringing such injustice to spill out on other species, exploiting them as mere resources, cornering them in ever scanter areas, or simply eradicating them, like the colonized peoples of the Earth. It is the well-known story of ambition, war, conquest, and submission of other peoples (often in God's name, under the guise of evangelization or civilization), brought now to a horrifying scale across the planet, wiping out entire species, in the name of development or progress.

The cry of the poor has become the cry of the Earth. Now, this is indeed "the last hour" (1 Jn 2:18ad), for if we do not pay heed to those cries nor repent from our exploitative ways, our species will meet the same end we inflict upon others. Earth is saturated with the blood of the innocent, spilled since the rise of human "civilization." The planet cries out to God for judgment and deliverance (Gn 4:10–11). It awaits the manifestation of the children of God to make things right by God's will, for abundant life to blossom again (Rm 8:19–22).

When Many Leave

In what First John deemed to be the last hour of his community, many had gone out from its ranks, leaving brothers and sisters behind to fend for themselves. Ever since that original schism in the Johannine community, recorded in 1 Jn 2:18–19, the church has had to live through many schisms, with Christian brothers and sisters breaking away from the fellowship. While we continue to pray and act toward a greater Christian unity among the churches, all Christian denominations are increasingly subject to a greater loss in numbers due to the secular wave that unfurls from the global north through the global south.

In the United States—a bastion of religiosity among so-called developed nations—younger generations are disaffiliating from the faith of their parents and grandparents. In 2023, 28 percent of US adults are now religiously unaffiliated, up twelve points from 16 percent in 2007, the Pew Research Center reported.[7] The majority (69 percent) of these unaffiliated nones are under fifty years old. Secularism is gaining on younger generations even in the United States.

According to another 2023 survey by the Pew Research Center,[8] about 20 percent of US adults identify themselves as Catholic, down 4 percent from the 24 percent recorded in 2007. Fifty-seven percent of US Catholics are white and 33 percent are Hispanic. The latter are younger: 57 percent below fifty years old, compared to 32 percent among white Catholics. However, even among Hispanic Catholics, the youth are disaffiliating. In a 2022 survey by the Pew Research Center,[9] the ratio of US Hispanics that identified as Catholic went down to 43 percent from the 67 percent recorded in 2010. At the same time, the ratio of nones went up 20 percent among Hispanics in the same period, largely between the ages of eighteen and twenty-nine, which means that younger generations are leaving the church of their parents and grandparents.

If younger generations leave Christian fellowship, they may not have found either abundant life in church life or inspiring and articulate witnesses to the faith among their elders.[10] They may have found humanist or ecological values and ideas more

---

[7] Pew Research Center, "Religious 'Nones' in America: Who They Are and What They Believe," January 24, 2024, https://pewrsr.ch/3SedVTm.

[8] Justin Nortey, Patricia Tevington, and Gregory A. Smith, "10 Facts about U.S. Catholics," Pew Research Center, March 4, 2025, https://pewrsr.ch/3VRqirS.

[9] Pew Research Center, "Among U.S. Latinos, Catholicism Continues to Decline but Is Still the Largest Faith," April 13, 2023, https://pewrsr.ch/3Uws0fE.

[10] This is why the word of advice from 1 Pt 3:15b should inspire a renewed sense of urgency in adult faith formation: "Always be ready to give an explanation to anyone who asks you for a reason for your hope."

appealing, or they may consider themselves "spiritual but not religious." Certainly, globalized secularity is a new framework of the mind that makes it more difficult to embrace the worldview of traditional faiths.[11] Alternatively, the lures of the secular world may be too strong for the seed of the gospel to grow to maturity in young people's hearts. Millennials and Generation Z in particular grow disconnected from human fellowship in the flesh, absorbed by their smartphones and social media networks.[12] If all they saw, heard, touched, and otherwise experienced was a culturally degraded form of Christianity—commerce galore and decorations on Christmas, Mardi Gras without Lent, chocolate bunnies for Easter—then there might have been too little substance to nurture their souls. The public scandal of sexual abuse by a number of clerics would suffice to erode trust in the church. Whatever the reasons, young people leaving in significant numbers is cause for sadness, pastoral concern, and discernment for those who stay.

Even among those who have stayed behind in the pews, how many have left in spirit? How many are informed, ordinary community-building Christian folk, invested in prayer, active mission, and passing on what they have received? Attendance numbers don't tell the whole story. The consistent drop in vo-

---

[11] To understand the worldwide phenomenon of secularity from its inception, see philosopher Charles Taylor's masterpiece *A Secular Age* (Belknap, 2007). A brief introduction for Catholics from the author himself is "A Catholic Modernity?" in *Dilemmas and Connections: Selected Essays* (Belknap, 2011). From a sociological point of view, see José Casanova's *Public Religions in the Modern World* (University of Chicago Press, 1994), esp. chapter 7 as a case study of Catholicism in the United States.

[12] See the comprehensive picture of that next generation (born 1995–2012), drawn from data and interviews by San Diego State University professor of psychology Jean M. Twenge, *iGen: Why Today's Super-Connected Kids Are Growing Up Less Rebellious, More Tolerant, Less Happy—And Completely Unprepared for Adulthood* (Atria Paperback, 2017), esp. chapter 5, on irreligiosity.

cations to the religious life or to parish ministry may be more telling.[13]

Beyond parish life and Christian fellowship, a more radical disengagement from the fate of the poor and the fate of the Earth is at stake. Ignorance and indifference grow toward entire populations of disenfranchised people. The lives of four billion people struggling for a livelihood at less than seven dollars a day simply do not count to the rich among us. Generations of poor people in the global south live and die in the fields or in sweatshops to provide low-cost produce, manufactured goods, and other commodities to the global north. However, the cost of these commodities is anything but low, for they come at the expense of the poor's own lives. Migrants seeking asylum at a country's borders are perceived as a threat, instead of desperate people looking for a safer, better future. We grow accustomed to the new normal of hotter weather, barren landscapes, and disappearing wildlife.

Meanwhile, millions of eyes turn hypnotically to the screens as the first billionaire pays for his own *private spacewalk*, 435 miles above the Earth.[14] Instead, why not donate those hundreds of millions of dollars for a *community walk* in some of the world's most overcrowded and poorly served slums? Space is the ultimate border that keeps humanity together with other living species on Earth. It is both telling and appalling that so many people—inspired by Hollywood movies that make millions of dollars of profits off our drifting minds—daydream about *leaving* this Earth for another planet, *leaving* the rest of us behind.[15]

---

[13] See the 2012 CARA report on the USCCB website, "Survey of Youth and Young Adults on Vocations," accessed September 12, 2024, usccb.org.

[14] Georgina Rannard, "Billionaire Completes First Private Spacewalk," BBC News, September 12, 2024.

[15] Thomas G. Hermans-Webster, "The Dystopic Relations of *Interstellar*: A Response from Christian Ecotheology," in *Theology, Religion, and Dystopia*, ed. Scott Donahue-Martens and Brandon Simonson (Lexington / Fortress Academic, 2022).

Remaining True to Our Calling

Remaining grounded on Earth and within our biosphere is a good start for our creaturely community, and connecting with our communities begins by attending gatherings and getting to know our neighbors. Building up the joy of fellowship, however, is so much more than just occupying an empty space in the pews. Christians are the anointed followers of the Anointed One, Jesus Christ. What was he anointed for? What were we anointed for? The evangelist Luke reminds us, with Jesus's reading of Isaiah:

> The Spirit of the Lord is upon me, because he has anointed me to bring glad tidings to the poor. He has sent me to proclaim liberty to captives and recovery of sight to the blind, to let the oppressed go free, and to proclaim a year acceptable to the Lord. (Lk 4:18–19; Is 61:1–2)

In my humble view, this text should be the very first lesson for catechumens. What is a Christian? An anointed person like Jesus Christ. What is anointing? Consecration for a mission. What mission? To bring good news to the poor; to take away the yoke of the oppressed; to illumine the lives of the downtrodden with God's hope; and to proclaim that such liberation is a holy priority, the use of our time that is acceptable to the Lord.

This concept is not difficult, but following through is. As First John points out, Christians need no special teaching aside from this truth of their anointing (2:27). By extending God's mercy to our neighbors in need, we are actively participating in the fellowship of the Father and the Son that brings forth enduring life (2:25). To deny the importance of this work of mercy is actually to negate the anointing of the Son of God and our own anointing (2:23). Indeed, some people would rather have Christians believe something different and get busy doing something that would not disturb their profitable business or their peace of mind. These are deceivers, *antichrists*, literally: opposed to the anointing that prioritizes the poor above anything else in the world (2:22, 26).

The gospel is in fact quite simple; we just need to remember that message, anointing, and mission, which was entrusted to us from the beginning of our faith (2:21, 24). It is a precious gift: the way to enjoy enduring life (2:25), with one another, with creation, and with God. If we get better at remembering and *remaining* in that word (2:28) through action, then maybe the joy of our fellowship will become attractive to those who have left.

5

Becoming Who We Are Called to Be

2:29 If you consider that he is righteous, you also know that everyone who acts in righteousness is begotten by him.

3:1 See what love the Father has bestowed on us that we may be called the children of God. Yet so we are. The reason the world does not know us is that it did not know him. **2** Beloved, we are God's children now; what we shall be has not yet been revealed. We do know that when it is revealed we shall be like him, for we shall see him as he is. **3** Everyone who has this hope based on him makes himself pure, as he is pure. **4** Everyone who commits sin commits lawlessness, for sin is lawlessness. **5** You know that he was revealed to take away sins, and in him there is no sin. **6** No one who remains in him sins; no one who sins has seen him or known him. **7** Children, let no one deceive you. The person who acts in righteousness is righteous, just as he is righteous. **8** Whoever sins belongs to the devil, because the devil has sinned from the beginning. Indeed, the Son of God was revealed to destroy the works of the devil. **9** No one who is begotten by God commits sin, because God's seed remains in him; he cannot sin because he is begotten by God. **10** In this way, the children of God and the children of the devil are made plain; no one who fails to act in righteousness belongs to God, nor anyone who does not love his brother.

1 Jn 2:29–3:10

In the preceding section, the author inspired his readers to remain rooted in their anointing in the aftermath of so many members leaving the fellowship. Now he is going to make plain what marks off those who remain faithful to their calling: acting righteously, keeping away from sin, becoming pure, becoming children of God ever more in the image of their Father, like Jesus the Son. In many ways, this fourth section, A' (2:29–3:10), comes back to topics similar to the first one, A (1:5–2:7), where those who claim to abide in God must keep God's commandments and walk under God's light, like Jesus did. The author's argument is cyclical. He presents that first basic idea of a life coherent with belief in the opening and then moves to reinforce it at the end of the first part of the letter (1:5–3:10). In between, he asserted the *passing* of the world order, B (2:8–17) and the call to *remain* faithful to God, B' (2:18–28), topics that are related by contrast.[1]

A stark contrast between those who belong to God and those who belong to the evil power at work in the world frames this

---

[1] A full chart of the recurring vocabulary that supports this ABB'A' arrangement of the first diptych in the letter's structure is given in the appendix.

section by *inclusio*.² Two ways of life are laid out: acting in righteousness shows our divine begetting (2:29b), while failing to do so reveals an allegiance to worldliness that brings about evil works (3:10ab). The very last clause of 3:10c announces the topic of love that is coming next.

The Train of Thought in 2:29–3:10

Verse 2:29 (A) establishes the main correlation between righteous actions and begetting by God. The just God is the source of all justice. All who seek justice and do what is just reveal their origin in God. This prompts the author's parenthetical exclamation in 3:1, regarding the astounding love that God has bestowed upon humans to call them God's children. Whoever misses out on this dignity has not known God as the author and his fellowship have.

The detailed argument of the section is presented twice, each time in the same order.³ It is easier to visualize the recurring vocabulary (*in italics*) that structures the argument in the following table:

---

² Noted by Duane F. Watson, *The Letters of John* (Cambridge University Press, 2024), 80.

³ Most commentators notice the recurring pattern of antitheses, formed by "everyone who" and "no one who" statements. So Watson, *The Letters of John*, 80–81; Judith M. Lieu, *I, II, & III John: A Commentary* (Westminster John Knox Press, 2008), 117–18; George Parsenios, *First, Second, and Third John* (Baker, 2014), 92; John Painter, *1, 2, and 3 John*, Sacra Pagina 18 (Liturgical, 2002), 226. Few, however, pick up on the recurrent vocabulary in sequence, from 3:2–6 to 3:7–9, that structures the argument. See Hans-Joseph Klauck, *Der erste Johannesbrief* (Benzinger, 1991), 190; Giorgio Giurisato, *Struttura e teologia de la Prima lettera di Giovanni* (Pontificio Istituto Biblico, 1998), 443–46.

B	3:2. Beloved, we are *God's children* now; what we shall be has not yet been revealed. We do know that when it is revealed we shall be like him, for we shall see him as he is.	B'	3:7a *Children*, let no one deceive you.
C	3:3 Everyone who has this hope based on him makes himself *pure, as he is pure*.	C'	3:7b The person who acts in righteousness is *righteous, just as he is righeous*.
D	3:4 *Everyone who commits sin* commits lawlessness, for *sin* is lawlessness.	D'	3:8a *Whoever sins* belongs to the devil, because the devil has *sinned* from the beginning.
E	3:5a You know that *he was revealed* to take away sins,	E'	3:8b Indeed, *the Son of God was revealed* to destroy the works of the devil.
F	3:5b and *in him there is no sin.* 3:6 *No one who remains in him sins*; no one who sins has seen him or known him.	F'	3:9 *No one who is begotten by God commits sin*, because God's seed *remains in him; he cannot sin* because he is begotten by God.

Units B-B' address the readers as children of God, a dignity presently held, yet called to develop into its full potential by not letting anyone lead them astray (B') and by yearning for the full revelation of God in the end (B). This highlights the parenetic nature of the argument: God's children are called to grow into their bestowed dignity.

Units C-C' reminds believers of the necessary conformity to Christ. Although the NABRE keeps the ambiguous pronoun "he," the actual pronoun in Greek is "that one" (*ekeinos*), always referring to Jesus, as it did in 2:6 and will do so again in 3:16. Jesus is pure (C) and righteous (C'). Believers are encouraged to be "just as" (*kathōs*) Jesus was among us.

Units D-D' show the origin of sin in the devil, who sinned from the beginning (D'), introducing lawlessness into the world (D)—an obvious allusion to the lies of the serpent in Genesis 3.

Units E-E' recall Jesus's divinely appointed mission to "destroy the works of the devil" (E') and to "take away sins" (E), restoring our relationship with God.

The argument in units F-F' is more difficult to grasp, mainly because of the ambiguity of the pronouns therein and the obscure reference to "God's seed." The basic idea is that believers do not sin, in that they keep communion with Jesus and God, since no sin is to be found in God. The detailed reasons in 3:9 (F') are murky and problematic, but an alternative translation and interpretation is offered later in this chapter.[4]

At the end of the section, verse 3:10 (A') concludes antithetically. Actions show the true origin of a person, whether it is in God or in evil. Readers are thus equipped to discern who may truly claim to know God or not. Readers are also made aware of the high moral standards they are called to live by if they are to honor their divine begetting. Lawlessness, injustice, and sin are incompatible with God, who is light, just, and merciful. They are unbecoming for God's true children.

---

[4] As the NABRE translation stands, this verse runs in direct contradiction with what the author stated previously in 1:8 and 1:10. According to these verses, *no one* can claim to be sinless. The NABRE's translation of 3:9 actually states that the righteous *cannot* commit sin anyway, because God's "seed" dwells in them (empowering them? protecting them? guiding them?).

Daughters and Sons of the Righteous

Children bear some physical resemblance to their parents, from whom they inherit those traits. Children also betray their parentage through character traits and learned behavior, modeled after their parents. This basic human experience is brought to bear on God-human relations. If humans claim to be God's children—to have their ultimate origin in God—then their behavior should tell the story of their true parentage.

No one has "seen" what God looks like (Jn 1:18a; 1 Jn 4:12a), yet God's character has been plainly revealed by Jesus, the Son of God (Jn 1:18b; 14:9; 1 Jn 1:1–3). If God is light and walks in the light (1 Jn 1:5, 7), so does Jesus (1 Jn 2:6). If God is faithful and just (1 Jn 1:9; 2:29), so is Jesus, the Son of God (1 Jn 2:1; 3:7c). If God is clean, pure, and without sin (1 Jn 3:5b), then so is Jesus (1 Jn 3:3). Christ is the example whom all children of God should follow in order to claim such high parentage.

Acting in righteousness, doing what is just, and avoiding lawlessness and sin mark off God's spiritual progeny: children who pay heed to God's word, who are taught by God, who act accordingly, and can claim "to know him" (1 Jn 3:1d, 6). What does this mean in an age of unrestrained environmental destruction?

God loves and cares for all living beings—God's creation—not just human beings, nor by the same token just a few among them (Wi 11:24–26). Pope Francis reminds us,

> Every creature is the object of the Father's tenderness, who gives it its place in the world. Even the fleeting life of the least of beings is the object of his love, and in its few seconds of existence, God enfolds it with his affection.[5]

---

[5] Francis, *Laudato Si'*, no. 77.

If God feeds the ravens (Lk 12:24) and clothes flowers and grass (Mt 6:28–30), how could God's true children disregard the fate of so many species living on Earth? Notice how the psalmist recognizes the wondrous balance in the natural order as a manifestation of God's sense of justice:

> The eyes of all look hopefully to you;
> you give them their food in due season.
> You open wide your hand
> and satisfy the desire of every living thing.
> The Lord is just in all his ways,
> merciful in all his works. (Ps 145:15–17)

To prey irresponsibly on other creatures out of unchecked greed, for sport, or just because no current law protects them is sheer human hubris, a blatant sin of injustice toward God's creation. To drain the life out of entire ecosystems for mere profit, under the disguise of human development, is devious and devilish. The Earth cries out in its plight to all of us to become true daughters and sons of God, who is just.

Smoke from northern forest fires, the Amazon rainforest, bleached coral reefs from all over the seas, and melting glaciers in the poles raise their prayers to God that God's children may awaken to the devastation they unwittingly consent to or from which they benefit. These phenomena are triggered by the excessive burning of fossil fuels to satisfy human consumerism, especially in the global north. Individuals do not get to see the indirect impact of their energy consumption, their pressure on the market for exotic yet cheap fresh produce, or their fondness for constantly replacing commodity goods. Many live unaware of the impact of what they deem to be a legally earned and innocent lifestyle. Others vaguely intuit the danger, yet prefer to live eyes wide shut, leaving their rooted habits unquestioned and unexamined. Responsible science acts as a whistleblower, but questioning scientific findings becomes an all-too-easy way to divert human conscience from the moral demand to change lifestyles that are costly to the environment.

Indifference or helplessness is no Christian witness worthy of the name. The good news of the gospel calls for conversion and hope in God (1 Jn 3:3). Conversion and a well-placed hope[6] lead to the practice of justice that the Earth and the poor long for, set as a standard for the children of God by First John (1 Jn 2:29b; 3:7b).

Lawlessness Is the Fruit of Deceit

In verse 3:7a, the parenetic character of this section comes forth. The author pleads with his readers not to be deceived by those who would disengage from the practice of justice, on the basis of some ill-conceived belief that becoming children of God is all that mattered. The audience can already be called "children of God" (1 Jn 3:1b) because they are truly loved by God (1 Jn 3:1a). However, this is not a final state, as the author envisions an even closer resemblance to their heavenly Father, something that is yet to be revealed and can still be yearned for (1 Jn 3:2). The faithful who progress in their obedience to God's will actually move forward in their vision and understanding of who God is, thereby conforming themselves ever more to the likeness of their heavenly Father, like Jesus the Son (1 Jn 3:3).

Acting in righteousness (1 Jn 2:29b; 3:7b) is the path laid out for God's children, as it was to walk in the light, like Jesus,

---

[6] A secular or worldly mindset devaluates the Christian virtue of hope into mere expectation of success. Hope becomes dependent on the odds. Where the odds are slim, hope fades. Given the vast complexity of the world climate crisis, many despair and give up, feeling helpless. The gospel invites us to do what is right and to place our hope in God, not in our own strength or chances of success. Abraham was right to hope against all odds (Rm 4:18–22; Gn 15:2–6).

Becoming Who We Are Called to Be

in the first section of the letter (1 Jn 1:5–2:7). Just as there is no darkness in God whatsoever (1 Jn 1:5b), so can there be no place in God whatsoever for injustice and sin (1 Jn 3:5b). True fellowship with a just God requires purification from all sin and injustice (1 Jn 1:6–7, 9; 2:1–2; 3:3). Maintaining such fellowship implies doing what is right, accomplishing what is just, like Jesus the Just (1 Jn 2:1b; 3:7b).

Minimizing the importance of sin is an act of deception: self-deception when thinking one is above sin (1 Jn 1:8), and deception of others when concealing the truth about injustice done unto others (1 Jn 1:10; 3:7a, 8, 10). Ultimately, one reveals or betrays one's true allegiance through one's choices and actions.

According to Johannine thought, an evil orientation is characterized by lies and deceit, "because the devil has sinned from the beginning" (1 Jn 3:8b). "He was a murderer from the beginning and does not stand in truth, because there is no truth in him. When he tells a lie, he speaks in character, because he is a liar and the father of lies" (Jn 8:44bc). Conversely, to do what is right one must forgo concealment and darkness, stepping into the light of God's truth.

It is no wonder that corporate interests often dictate lines of communication that conceal rather than reveal the truth that would compromise their investments. The oil industry denied global warming, just as the tobacco companies denied the relationship between smoking and cancer, or agribusiness hides its lethal impact on the environment. Consumers in the global north do not see firsthand the ravages of extractive economies in the global south, managed by transnational corporations that keep the producer and the consumer apart. The poor in those countries work on unlivable wages and under unlivable conditions only to see their local resources plundered free of tax. Liberal economies insist on an absolutely "free market," "unregulated" to ensure "development": a lie thrown to the faces of all who endure the plundering, without ever enjoying the comforts of the "developed" world.

First John's word for "unregulated" is "lawlessness" (*anomia*), and it is a sin (1 Jn 3:4), for it spreads and normalizes injustice (*adikia*), the work of the devil (1 Jn 3:8c).

God's Seed

As hinted at earlier, verses 3:5–9 contain ambiguous and problematic statements. They would appear to convey the idea that Christians no longer sin, protected, guided, or strengthened by a divine power that dwells in them: God's seed. The idea that the baptized are immune henceforth from sin is un-Christian. One might even call sinlessness a heresy, invalidated by daily experience, as well as by other New Testament texts, starting with the very first chapter of First John:

> If we say, "We are without sin," we deceive ourselves, and the truth is not in us.
> If we acknowledge our sins, he is faithful and just and will forgive our sins and cleanse us from every wrongdoing. If we say, "We have not sinned," we make him a liar, and his word is not in us. (1 Jn 1:8–10)

How, then, can the same author state in chapter 3, "No one who remains in him sins" (1 Jn 3:6a)? And furthermore,

> No one who is begotten by God commits sin,
> because God's seed remains in him;
> he cannot sin because he is begotten by God.
> (1 Jn 3:9)

Commentators have dealt with this striking contradiction in various ways. Attributing verse 3:9 to another source is a theory that is no longer upheld.⁷ Grammatical subtlety allows for a distinction between "habitual" sin (present tense, as in 3:9) and occasional sin (aorist or perfect tense, as in 1:10): Christians may occasionally sin, but they no longer lead a life of sin.⁸ Understanding "lawlessness" (*anomia*) in 3:4 not as everyday immorality but as the final (eschatological) clash between God and the forces of evil would call for taking "sin" in 3:6–9 as referring specifically to apostasy or violent opposition to God, an evil that Christians do not embrace, even when they occasionally fail to live by God's justice.⁹

This is where recognizing the parallelism between verses 3:5–6 and 3:8b–9 may turn out to be helpful. Distinguishing between pronouns is key: "that one" (*ekeinos*) stands for Jesus (cf. 1 Jn 2:6; 3:16), whereas "him" (*autos*) may actually refer to God. The clause "he cannot sin" in 3:9c may state a prohibition, not an incapacity: Christians "cannot sin" in the sense that they "must not / should not sin," even though we are quite capable of it, and we often do.¹⁰ Finally, "God's seed" (*sperma theou*) need not be a power conferred to Christians, but actually designate Christians themselves as God's children.¹¹ Taken together, these

---

[7] See Rudolf Bultmann, *The Johannine Epistles* (Fortress, 1973), 52.

[8] So think Daniel L. Akin, *1, 2, 3 John* (B&H, 2001), 142–43; Painter, *1, 2, and 3 John*, 227–28.

[9] So Rudolf Schnackenburg, *The Johannine Epistles* (Crossroad, 1992), 170–72; Raymond E. Brown, *The Epistles of John*, Anchor Bible 30 (Doubleday, 1982), 398–400, 427–28; Robert W. Yarbrough, *1–3 John* (Baker Academic, 2008), 181–83.

[10] The verb *dynamai* (can/cannot) is likewise used with the imperative sense in Mt 9:15; Mk 2:19; Lk 5:34; Acts 4:16, 20; 10:47; 25:11; 1 Cor 10:21. Stephen S. Smalley, *1, 2, 3 John* (Word, 1984), 161–63, speaks of sinlessness as a "Christian obligation," not a "realized truth." Whence the summons to "become what you are," as Ian H. Marshall, *The Epistles of John* (Eerdmans, 1978), 183, would put it. Hence the title of this chapter: "Becoming Who We Are Called to Be."

[11] As in "the seed of Abraham," i.e., "the descendants of Abraham" in Jn 8:33, 37. So think Alan E. Brooke, *A Critical and Exegetical Commentary on*

choices yield another translation, provided next in parallel form. For clarity, I have replaced the ambiguous expressions and the pronouns with the new referential choices:

E	3:5a You know that *Jesus was revealed to take* away sins,	E'	3:8b Indeed, *the Son of God was revealed* to destroy the works of the devil.
F	3:5b and *in God there is no sin.* 3:6 *No one who remains in God sins*; no one who sins has seen God or known God.	F'	3:9 *No one who is begotten by God commits sin*, because a child of God *remains in God*; he *must not sin* because he is begotten by God.

This translation dispels the apparent contradiction with 1:8–10. The author of First John is not clearing Christians of their responsibility to walk under the light of God's justice, nor is he reassuring them that, with some divine power at work, they would be immune to sin, be it the word of God or the Spirit of God, or their baptismal anointing. First John is emphatically calling his flock to abide in God,[12] avoid sin, and strive to live in God's justice. The whole section of 2:29–3:10 is built upon the contrast of those who may claim to be God's seed, God's children, and those who cannot make such claim because they

---

the Johannine Epistles (T&T Clark, 1964), 89; Bultmann, *Johannine Epistles*, 52; Yarbrough, *1–3 John*, 193–95; Jeff de Waal Dryden, "The Sense of σπέρμα in 1 John 3:9 in Light of Lexical Evidence," *Filología neotestamentaria* 11 (1998): 85–100.

[12] Some scholars point out that inasmuch as they abide in God, Christians do not sin, an interpretation going back to Bede and Augustine. See Brooke, *Johannine Epistles*, 86; Bultmann, *Johannine Epistles*, 51; James L. Houlden, *A Commentary on the Johannine Epistles* (Adam & Charles Black, 1973), 94; Watson, *The Letters of John*, 90, 94.

do not reflect righteousness in their lives—the distinctive trait of God's family.

The Earth and the poor suffer from "lawlessness." The resources needed to support life are up for grabs, and "might makes right" seems to be the only rule allowed to stand. Worse, the rich and powerful disguise their sin and pretend to be virtuous providers of work and development for the human race. Some may even masquerade by offering pious prayers and donations to the poor, while keeping in their grasp full control of the market, the Earth's resources, and the fate of the poor. First John calls for discernment:

> Children, let no one deceive you. The person who acts in righteousness is righteous, just as he is righteous. (1 Jn 3:7)

Only actions and their real outcome reveal the human heart. However imperfect our steps toward justice for all may be, we grow into the likeness of the Father and Creator of all with each movement. We become ever more the true children of a generous, life-giving, and just God.

6

Opening Our Hearts

~

3:11 For this is the message you have heard from the beginning: we should love one another, **12** unlike Cain who belonged to the evil one and slaughtered his brother. Why did he slaughter him? Because his own works were evil, and those of his brother righteous. **13** Do not be amazed, [then,] brothers, if the world hates you. **14** We know that we have passed from death to life because we love our brothers. Whoever does not love remains in death.

15 Everyone who hates his brother is a murderer, and you know that no murderer has eternal life remaining in him. **16** The way we came to know love was that he laid down his life for us; so we ought to lay down our lives for our brothers. **17** If someone who has worldly means sees a brother in need and refuses him compassion, how can the love of God remain in him? **18** Children, let us love not in word or speech but in deed and truth.

19 [Now] this is how we shall know that we belong to the truth and reassure our hearts before him **20** in whatever our hearts condemn, for God is greater than our hearts and knows everything. **21** Beloved, if [our] hearts do not condemn us, we have confidence in God **22** and receive from him whatever we ask, because we keep his commandments and do what pleases him. **23** And his commandment is this: we should believe in the name of his Son, Jesus Christ, and love one another just as he commanded us.

1 Jn 3:11–23

We come to the second part of the letter, introduced by the key leading sentence: "For this is the message you have heard from the beginning" (1 Jn 3:11a). The wording recalls the beginning of the first part: "Now this is the message that we have heard from him and proclaim to you" (1 Jn 1:5a). In the first part, the message was that "God is light" (1 Jn 1:5b). Readers were called to walk in the light like Jesus (1 Jn 1:7; 2:6)—to do what is just, like him (1 Jn 3:7). Now, in the second part, the message is more specific: to love one another (1 Jn 3:11b), like Jesus loved us (1 Jn 3:16). We are delving deeper into what it means to accept the light of God in our lives. True light and justice are revealed to be love in action. So now, throughout the second part of the letter, the author revisits points already made. By doing so, the author can drive home the consequences of accepting the truths that the first part of the letter lays out.

Just as 1 John 2:8–17 introduced the topic of love of the brethren, contrasting it with the way the world pretends to love—covetousness and boastfulness (1 Jn 2:15–17)—now it is time for First John to expound on what true love really is.

The Train of Thought in 3:11–23

Verses 11–12a (unit A) and verse 23 (unit A′) clearly frame this section by *inclusio*,[1] focusing on the love commandment at the heart of the gospel message. They also set the contrast between Cain and Jesus that this section develops.

A	3:11 For *this* is the message you have heard from the beginning: *we should love one another*, 3:12a unlike Cain	A′	3:23 And *this* is his commandment: *we should* believe in the name of his Son, *Jesus Christ*, and *love one another* just as he commanded us.

Verses 12b–15 (unit B) and 17–22 (unit B′) run parallel to each other. They form the body of the section, illustrating very graphically what it means *not to love* one another "in deed and truth" (3:18). On the one side (unit B), bad choices and resentment toward one's brother lead to murder, like Cain slaying Abel in Genesis 4,[2] forgoing enduring life. On the other side (unit B′), closing one's heart to the needs of brothers and sisters amounts to slaughtering them, no different an act than Cain's murder of

---

[1] Noticed as well by Duane F. Watson, *The Letters of John* (Cambridge University Press, 2024), 95; following Raymond E. Brown, *The Epistles of John* (Doubleday, 1982), 467. D. F. Watson adds verse 3:24 to round off the section, because he considers direct address in 4:1 ("Beloved") to be the marker of a new section. It is preferable to give precedence to lexical boundaries: verse 3:24 introduces the topic of the Spirit, which is the hallmark of the following section, 3:24–4:13.

[2] This is the only explicit reference to Scripture in the letter, something quite indicative of its importance. This passage has been studied among other Jewish *aggadoth* (rereading interpretations) by Frederick D. Eluvathingal, *An*

his brother Abel. Enduring life (*zōē aiōnios*) cannot be enjoyed if we keep our livelihood (*bios*) to ourselves, closing our hearts (literally, guts: *splanchna*, 3:17) to the suffering of others. Strongly put, *not opening our guts* on behalf of others inevitably leads to *opening their guts*—that is, slaughtering our brothers and sisters. Self-centeredness begets indifference, which ends up costing other people's lives. Whatever we consent to lose on behalf of others, we can ask God, and we may rest assured of God's mercy (3:19–22).[3] Compassion begets compassion.

Verse 16ab (units C-C′) forms the very center of this section, laying out the example of our Lord Jesus, who selflessly laid down his own life (*psychē*) for us.[4] The section pivots from hateful inclinations (unit B) to livelihood sharing (unit B′) through the example of Christ, who taught us "in deed and truth" that love is always offering ourselves to others (C-C′):

Exegetical Inquiry into 1 John 3:11–18: Aggadah of Cain and Abel in the New Testament and in Early Judaism (Studium Biblicum Franciscanum, 2010).

[3] These verses harbor many textual and grammatical problems that obscure their meaning, a puzzle that George L. Parsenios, *First, Second, and Third John* (Baker Academic, 2014), 104, likens to solving a Rubik's cube. Judith M. Lieu, *I, II, & III John* (Westminster John Knox, 2008), 154–56, summarizes well the alternatives. For an extensive discussion, see Brown, *Epistles*, 453–60. Brown wisely points out that in the end, all boils down to whether "the verses speak of the severity or the mercy of God," something that cannot be decided "through grammar alone" but is based on immediate context and "the general outlook of the epistolary author" (459–60). Although First John contains warnings and statements of reassurance, the latter seem to better fit the immediate context, a sentiment reflected in the NABRE translation adopted here.

[4] The language of "laying down" (*tithēmi*) one's personal life *(psychē)* like one sheds a garment is reminiscent of the washing of the disciples' feet in Jn 13:4. The humble washing foreshadows Jesus's dying for each one of them, as foretold in the shepherd's discourse in Jn 10:11, 15, 17, 18. Simon Peter claims he will reciprocate in Jn 13:37–38. The same language is taken up in Jn 15:12–13, illustrating the love commandment, like it does here in 1 Jn 3:16.

| C | 3:16a The way we came to know love was that he laid down his life for us; | C' | 3:16b so we ought to lay down our lives for our brothers. |

One might even venture that verse 3:16 is the theological pivot of the entire letter. It sums up what the Christian way and calling truly are in the paschal mystery. The fullest revelation of God's love, justice, and mercy towards us shines in its brightest light upon the cross. Only from that vantage point do the themes of light, faith, justice, and love receive their fairest treatment. Only at the foot of the cross may our divine begetting and our holy anointing be fully understood. True joy and fellowship must somehow flow, like enduring life, from Christ's pierced side.

To Love after Jesus

Jesus's death on a Roman cross is interpreted by First John as a willful self-sacrifice for the sake (*hyper*) of others. The author includes his epistolary audience and himself ("for us," 3:16a) among the beneficiaries of this selfless act. He further underscores that this is how Christians came to know what love is and how they ought to love one another. By dying on our behalf, Jesus raises us to the dignity of being his brothers and sisters, worthy of his loss of personal life (*psychē*). Even all those whom Jesus of Nazareth never knew directly in flesh and blood—starting with the first audience of the letter—are included in the loving embrace of his arms as they are stretched out on the cross.

To lay down one's life on behalf of others out of love is certainly the ultimate sacrifice, the highest and noblest expression of a love that is no empty talk but love "in deed and truth." Yet laying down one's life is also the most consequent behavior—however daunting—for a disciple of Jesus. At this point, it is worth quoting the Fourth Gospel in full on the topic:

> As the Father loves me, so I also love you.
> Remain in my love.
> If you keep my commandments, you will remain
> in my love,
> just as I have kept my Father's commandments
> and remain in his love.
> I have told you this so that my joy may be in you
> and your joy may be complete.
> This is my commandment: love one another as I
> love you.
> No one has greater love than this, to lay down
> one's life for one's friends.
> You are my friends if you do what I command
> you. (Jn 15:9–14)

From this passage, it becomes clear that John and First John speak of covenantal love.[5] This is a love that springs forth from God's bosom as Father (Jn 1:18; 1 Jn 4:10–12). This love is poured onto the Son, and, from him, it spreads unto God's children (Jn 15:9). God yearns to establish a covenantal relationship between God and God's children, through Jesus. God teaches God's children how to love through Jesus's life example. *Just as* Jesus remains joyfully obedient to God, ever remaining in the Father's embrace (Jn 15:10b–11), *so does* Jesus bid his disciples to remain in his friendly embrace by becoming obedient to him

---

[5] See Rekha M. Chennattu, *Johannine Discipleship as Covenantal Relationship* (Hendrickson, 2006). For a comparative analysis of the language of love in the Gospel and the letter, see Fernando F. Segovia, *Love Relationships in the Johannine Tradition: Agapē/Agapan in I John and the Fourth Gospel* (Scholars, 1982). The call to remain in Jesus's love is best understood within the covenantal framework, whence the invitation to keep the commandments. See Edward Malatesta, *Interiority and Covenant: A Study of* εἶναι ἐν *and* μένειν ἐν *in the First Letter of Saint John* (Biblical Institute, 1978).

and loving one another *as he did* (Jn 15:10a, 12, 14). If verse 13 sets the love standard as high as Jesus's self-sacrifice, verse 11 assures of the fullness of joy that comes with it.

Evidently, no ill or menace looms over this course of action in Johannine thought. It is no mere coincidence that "complete joy" was stated as the ultimate purpose for writing First John (1:4). From the beginning of the letter, the author knew exactly where he was going to lead his readers and place the Christian hope for true and everlasting joy: at the foot of the cross.

One may not quite yet be cheerful enough to part with one's life for the sake of others. To build up enough joy for that, the learning curve is steep, but daily training in fellowship is readily available. Parting with some of our possessions to help others in need and showing them compassion is a little bit like learning to die for others, step by step. Saint Augustine clearly saw this when he read 1 Jn 3:17 and preached on it:

> Look, this is where charity begins. If you aren't yet ready to die for your brother, be ready to give of your goods to your brother. Let charity strike your heart now, so that you don't act for the sake of display but out of mercy's inmost marrow, so that you consider him as the one who is suffering want. For, if you can't give what is superfluous to your brother, how can you lay down your life for your brother?[6]

For John as well as for Augustine, it appears that charity is the school for martyrdom, the accessible means for us to learn how to love after Jesus's example. We may not always face the need for the ultimate witness of faith, martyrdom, but we face the unmet needs of others every day. Pope Francis teaches, "If I can help at least one person to have a better life, that already justifies the

---

[6] Augustine, *Homilies on the First Epistle of John*, trans. Boniface Ramsey (New City, 2008), 85. The excerpt is taken from homily 5, paragraph 12.

offering of my life."[7] In a world plagued by systemic injustice and an appalling disparity of means among humans across the planet, only charitable goodwill may bridge the social chasms of our creation.

This is not to say that injustice should prevail so that charity may abound; to paraphrase St. Paul: "of course not!" (Rom 6:1). We must uncover and dismantle the systems of oppression that keep our fellow humans from earning a decent livelihood and that prevent them from flourishing on their own terms. We might actually be profiting from those systems ourselves—in which case, raising our voices against them, casting our vote against them, and tearing them down would entail parting with some of our possessions and privileges to provide relief, fair treatment, and opportunity to others.

A love that truly cares for the other does not end with a simple act of charity, although this may be the first step. "It is an equally indispensable act of love to strive to organize and structure society so that one's neighbor will not find himself in poverty."[8] Laws, ideas, and systems that "allow our brothers and sisters to die of hunger and thirst, without shelter or access to health care" must be reviewed and changed out of justice and love.[9] Following Christ's commitment to bettering the lives of the poor, we who claim to be his disciples must see to it that this task is done in our place and time.

"If someone who has worldly means sees a brother in need and refuses him compassion," the verse reads (1 Jn 3:17). The key is to see the other, and to acknowledge him as a brother, to welcome her as a sister. Even if the language of fraternity was

---

[7] Pope Francis, Apostolic Exhortation *Evangelii Gaudium*, 274; Encyclical Letter *Fratelli Tutti*, 195.

[8] Pontifical Council for Justice and Peace, *Compendium of the Social Doctrine of the Church*, 208; quoted by Pope Francis in his 2020 Encyclical Letter *Fratelli Tutti*, 186.

[9] Pope Francis, Encyclical Letter *Fratelli Tutti*, 87.

primarily used to designate members of the Johannine fellowship or of the Christian churches at large—a sort of extended family by divine begetting, God's family[10]—the love for the brethren must flow outward also unto all those for whom Christ laid down his life:

> He is expiation for our sins, and not for our sins only but for those of the whole world. (1 Jn 2:2)

Again, St. Augustine clearly saw here the connection between love of the brethren and the origin of all brotherhood and sisterhood in the sacrifice of Jesus Christ, who redeems all of humanity and binds us as family in his blood:

> Your brother is hungry, he is needy. Perhaps he is anxious and is being pressed by a creditor. He has nothing, you have something. He is your brother. You have been purchased together; your price is the same; both of you have been redeemed by the blood of Christ.[11]

Perhaps inevitably so, our natural sense of kinship runs at a much closer range, one limited by blood ties and a common gene pool. Family feuds can even take a toll on who may be treated like a son or a daughter, a brother or a sister. Unfortunately, modern Western individualism has made self-sufficiency an ideal state, encouraging us to put others at a distance, making us lose a sense of belonging, interdependence, and cooperation. We are now more inclined to sever ties than to welcome newcomers

---

[10] See Dirk G. Van der Merwe, "Family Metaphorics: A Rhetorical Tool in the Epistle of 1 John," *Acta Patristica et Byzantina* 20, no. 1 (2009): 89–108. More in depth: Jan G. Van der Watt, *Family of the King: Dynamics of Metaphor in the Gospel according to John* (Leiden, 2000), 304–22.

[11] Augustine, *Homilies on the First Epistle of John*, 85–86 (homily 5, paragraph 12).

and enlarge our tents. Fences and borders give us a false sense of safety and identity. Even our families shrink and shrivel. We learn to push the other aside, failing to see them as one of us.[12] How will we ever become sensitive to our ties to other living species—those distant relatives—if we do not take the first steps in acknowledging and treating *all* human beings as our brothers and sisters?

Life and Livelihood

The letter started with a bold witness to the life (*zōē*) that God has made available to us in Jesus Christ (1 Jn 1:2). Halfway through the letter, it becomes apparent that such enduring life (*zōē aiōnios*) is communicated through the laying down of the Son's personal life (*psychē*) out of love for us (1 Jn 3:16a). When we share our livelihood (*bios*) with others in need (1 Jn 3:17), we open our guts to brothers and sisters for whom Jesus shed his own blood. If he died so that we may all live, we walk in Jesus's footsteps (1 Jn 2:6) by showing compassion and solidarity with our extended fraternity, by parting with some of our life sustenance (*bios*) so that others may live. In doing so, we walk away from Cain's path of mundane coveting (1 Jn 2:16) that ended in violence and manslaughter (1 Jn 3:12). In the very act of sharing our livelihood (*bios*) with others, we demonstrate in our personal lives (*psychē*) and can rest assured that we have passed from death to the new life (*zōē*) gracefully given us (1 Jn 3:14). Because we love in deed and truth like Jesus (1 Jn 3:18), we know that the life-giving love of God remains in us (1 Jn 3:17c).

---

[12] Providentially—in the midst of a global pandemic—God has spoken to us of true fraternity in the words of God's servant, Pope Francis. A slow-paced, communal, and dialogical reading of his 2020 encyclical letter *Fratelli Tutti* is a good starting point to renew our sense of fraternity with all human beings, and to realize what this renewal entails.

Love in action is the clearest sign of the life of God abiding in us, because acts of love manifest the overflow of God's life and love in our hearts. Coveting, boasting, and hoarding show contempt for other people's lives; they amount to hatred (1 Jn 3:13, 15). In spite of appearances, protecting one's livelihood regardless of the needs of others does not keep us whole, nor does it secure life for anybody. Consumerism consumes us, and we pass away with the sad figure of this world (1 Jn 2:17). To the contrary, opening our hearts and putting our lives a little at risk for the sake of others make the life and love of God flow through our veins. We become whole by emptying ourselves, by opening our hearts to others, who thus become our brothers and sisters. In fellowship lies the wholesome life, not in isolation.

Life is a web of acts of love, not a thing to be possessed. We know we embrace the web of life when we let go and cling no more to our livelihood but share it with others. Life in our planet is based on the sharing of vital resources by all living species. We all breathe the same air, soak in the same sunlight, drink the same water, and stand on the same soil that countless generations of living creatures have for the past three billion years. The very atoms and molecules that form our bodies are nothing new that we might call our own: they formed other beings before and will do so again when we die and yield them up; we are made of recycled material! We are the new quilt that life has woven with the same old scraps of wool that once featured other patterns of life, each of them beautiful, priceless, and unique.

This is why it is so appalling to see the latest dominant species—humans—take over as if nothing else counted, not only looting landscapes and hoarding resources, but destroying well-balanced ecosystems and leaving Earth scorched, polluted, and barren. The one species with heightened rational capacities: to reflect, to recall, to calculate, to project itself into the future—we are the ones living as if there were no other species worth saving and no tomorrow.

When confronted with the crude facts of our behavior, we still resort to Cain's answer: "I do not know. Am I my brother's keeper?" (Gn 4:9). Yes! We are each others' keeper. We are also the keepers of God's beautiful garden (Gn 2:15). After taking the forbidden fruit out of sheer coveting, to boast on our God-like power and image (Gn 3), we have turned Eden into a desolate, artificial, and silent place, whence wildlife has been banned. We must learn to share land, air, water, and nutrients with other creatures, as well as with our human brothers and sisters. Life cannot endure when only one species thrives: the environment turns into a toxic wasteland. For a viable ecosystem to form and endure, life-forms need to acknowledge their interdependence and cooperate, not eliminate each other. For the sake of our own lives and those of our descendants, we must step down from our boasting pedestal and open our hearts to the precious lives of worms, fungi, and plants.[13]

God Is Greater Than Our Hearts

As we assess humanity's path from Cain down to our own times, we might be tempted to despair. The blood of Abel and of Jesus the Just has been spilled countless times throughout history. War and genocide have plagued relationships between human cultures that should have regarded each other as siblings. How often has the name of God been invoked against the other, hiding the truth that violence was unleashed to control territory and resources? How often have we hidden the people who are

---

[13] This is not an idyllic vision of a world cleansed of all predation, for predation, when measured, is also cleansing, bringing balance to the food chain of life. Unfortunately, humans mistake natural predation for a right to get rid of unwanted species and to raise their pets and favorite food beyond measure. Man's industrial farming and fishing are no Garden of Eden; they are signs of human hubris and contempt for the humble measure of natural processes.

mistreated as a mere labor force for a controlling minority's interests, not God's?

Nonetheless, we are not called to save the planet by astute planning, sheer will, or moral worth. We are called to enter the covenant of the living with the God of life, to practice sharing our livelihood as we grow in the love that spares other lives at the cost of one's own, and to have confidence in the commanding mercy of a God that knows infinitely better than us the path to harmony within the fellowship of the living.

7

Discerning God's Spirit in All Flesh

❧

3:24 Those who keep his commandments remain in him, and he in them, and the way we know that he remains in us is from the Spirit that he gave us.

4:1 Beloved, do not trust every spirit but test the spirits to see whether they belong to God, because many false prophets have gone out into the world. **2** This is how you can know the Spirit of God: every spirit that acknowledges Jesus Christ come in the flesh belongs to God, **3** and every spirit that does not acknowledge Jesus does not belong to God. This is the spirit of the antichrist that, as you heard, is to come, but in fact is already in the world. **4** You belong to God, children, and you have conquered them, for the one who is in you is greater than the one who is in the world. **5** They belong to the world; accordingly, their teaching belongs to the world, and the world listens to them. **6** We belong to God, and anyone who knows

God listens to us, while anyone who does not belong to God refuses to hear us. This is how we know the spirit of truth and the spirit of deceit.

7 Beloved, let us love one another, because love is of God; everyone who loves is begotten by God and knows God. **8** Whoever is without love does not know God, for God is love. **9** In this way the love of God was revealed to us: God sent his only Son into the world so that we might have life through him. **10** In this is love: not that we have loved God, but that he loved us and sent his Son as expiation for our sins. **11** Beloved, if God so loved us, we also must love one another. **12** No one has ever seen God. Yet, if we love one another, God remains in us, and his love is brought to perfection in us.

13 This is how we know that we remain in him and he in us, that he has given us of his Spirit.

1 Jn 3:24–4:13

Most commentators see a fresh start in 1 Jn 4:1. The author addresses the audience directly again, "Beloved," and turns their attention to the new topic of testing spirits.[1] Verses 1–6 do dwell on this topic and are to be kept together as a unit. The problem is how to make sense of the flow of ideas before and after that.

---

[1] I will not capitalize "spirit" in this chapter, unless it might refer to the Spirit of God, as it is done in the USCCB translation. In contrast with the Gospel, First John does not speak of God as Spirit (Jn 4:24), nor does it characterize God's Spirit as the Paraclete (Jn 14–16). Flesh is energized by spirit (Jn 6:63), but the phenomenon is equivocal, depending on where a spirit leads: truth or deceit (1 Jn 4:6c). Discernment is thus needed (1 Jn 4:1), lest one falls prey to the spirit of the antichrist (1 Jn 4:3).

Love is clearly a recurring topic in the second part of the letter (1 Jn 3:11–5:21). The previous section (1 Jn 3:11–23) recalled the commandment to love and the example of Jesus laying down his life for us out of love. Hence, verse 4:7 is not quite introducing the topic of love, "let us love one another," so much as it is weaving it into what precedes it. Direct address is no sure means of determining the start of a new section, since shortly after "Beloved" in 4:1, we have it again in 4:7 and in 4:11. Commentators who posit a new section on the topic of love starting at 4:7 hardly agree on where it might end.[2]

It is better to notice the striking reprise of key terms of verse 3:24 (unit A) in verse 4:13 (unit A′), forming an *inclusio* on divine indwelling and the gift of the Spirit. A careful survey of vocabulary yields interesting parallels on the sending of the Son between verses 4:1–6 (unit B) and 4:9–12 (unit B′), leaving the call to love in verses 4:7 (unit C) and 4:8 (unit C^{-1}) right at the center of the section. The issue is not to separate into two distinct sections the treatment of the topic of the spirit from the topic of love. Rather, we must see what connects them in the author's mind, within the boundaries set by the formal *inclusio*. Why address love and testing the spirits at the same time?

---

[2] The short cut is usually made at 4:21. So James L. Houlden, *A Commentary on the Johannine Epistles* (Adam & Charles Black, 1973), 112–21; John Painter, *1, 2, and 3 John*, Sacra Pagina 18 (Liturgical, 2002), 265–88; Kelly Anderson and Daniel Keating, *James, First, Second, and Third John*, Catholic Commentary on Sacred Scripture (Baker Academic, 2017), 209–21; George Parsenios, *First, Second, and Third John* (Baker, 2014), 114–18. The longer cut stretches to 5:4 or 5:5. See Rudolf Schnackenburg, *The Johannine Epistles* (Crossroad, 1992), 206–30; Raymond E. Brown, *The Epistles of John*, Anchor Bible 30 (Doubleday, 1982), 512–68; Stephen S. Smalley, *1, 2, 3 John* (Word, 1984), 232–72; Judith M. Lieu, *I, II, & III John: A Commentary* (Westminster John Knox Press, 2008), 175–204; Duane F. Watson, *The Letters of John* (Cambridge University Press, 2024), 114–30.

The Train of Thought in 3:24–4:13

The main idea framing this section at both ends (unit A 3:24 and unit A' 4:13) is our reception of the gift of God's Spirit, which becomes the foundational experience for knowing God and for living in intimate fellowship with God. Such covenantal intimacy is expressed in typically Johannine terms by mutual indwelling statements: we dwell in God, as much as God dwells in us.[3] Any discernment we make needs to be grounded deep in our spiritual experience.

A	3:24 Those who keep his commandments *remain in him, and he in them*, and the way we know that he remains in us is from the Spirit that he gave us.	A'	4:13 *This is how we know that we remain in him and he in us*, that he has given us of his Spirit.

This calls to mind Ezekiel's prophecy, whereby God's Spirit would guide and empower God's people to walk the path of salvation laid out for them, keeping God's commandments:

I will put my spirit within you so that you walk in my statutes, observe my ordinances, and keep them. (Ez 36:27)

The outward element of keeping God's commandments manifests the indwelling of God's Spirit in a person, which builds up knowledge of God as righteous, faithful, and true to his promise.

---

[3] The language is reminiscent of the Last Supper discourses in the Fourth Gospel: Jn 14–17, esp. Jn 14:20–21, 23; 15:4, 9–10; 17:20–23, 26. The gift of the Spirit introduces us into the inner life and fellowship of the Trinity.

Verses 4:1–6 form unit B, warning readers about the equivocal nature of spiritual indwelling, and so encouraging them to test the origin of a spirit, so as not to be deceived or misled by it.[4] Commentators see a Christological test in verses 4:2–3: confessing the incarnation of the Son of God is a sign of God's Spirit, whereas denying the incarnation gives away the spirit of the antichrist. This calls to mind Paul's advice to the Corinthians:

> Therefore, I tell you that nobody speaking by the spirit of God says, "Jesus be accursed." And no one can say, "Jesus is Lord," except by the holy Spirit. (1 Cor 12:3)

The second test in 4:4–6 is ecclesiological: listening to the Spirit of God is a communal or synodal experience of the people of God, not just an individual's personal flair or intuition. This is because the Spirit of God is a covenantal promise to the people of God, not an individual's privilege (see again Ez 36:27). Joining with others in God's family and discerning with and within the family of God is key to being grounded in God's truth.

Verses 4:9–12 form unit B′. Although these verses appear at first to be unrelated to verses 4:1–6 (unit B) because they now speak on the topic of love, careful examination of the vocabulary shows they run parallel to unit B. While 4:1–6 calls for discernment of the *origin* of spirits, 4:9–12 develops the *origin* of love. In both units, the *sending* and *coming* of God's Son are foundational for discernment. The following table displays the relevant recurring vocabulary.

---

[4] Duane F. Watson, *The Letters of John* (Cambridge University Press, 2024), 108–9, reviews and documents the different traditions behind such testing of spirits: the commonly held belief that humankind is subject to the influence of divine and diabolic spirits; the Old Testament instruction to test the prophets, who might be motivated by an evil spirit; and the expectation of the coming of false prophets in the end times.

B	4:1-6	B'	4:9-12
	Beloved This is how you can know This is how we can know		Beloved In this way ... was revealed to us In this is ...
	The *Spirit* of God		The *love* of God
	The one who is in you		God remains in us
	Jesus Christ come in the flesh		God sent his only Son ... and sent his Son
	many false prophets have gone out into the world the antichrist that ... is to come, but in fact is already in the world belongs to the world ... the world listens		... into the world

In spite of unit B dealing with the spirit of God and unit B' with the love of God, how could we miss the contrast between the coming of the false prophets and antichrists, their welcome hearing by the world, and the sending or coming of Christ the Son, rejected by the world? The incarnation reveals both the love of God bestowed upon us (B') and the true faith that the Spirit of God inspires (B). This is because God cares for all flesh—God's creation—and he sends his Son and his Spirit that we may live (4:9b). Conversely, the world welcomes false messiahs and prophets that sing the world's tune of indifference to the plight of flesh. This is why popularity is no sign of God's favor or of God's Spirit. Faith in Jesus Christ come in the flesh rules out any fake spirituality that disengages from care for the poor or for all living beings of God's creation.

At the heart of this section, verse 4:7 (unit C) and verse 4:8 (unit C^{-1}) articulate the call to love one another in covenantal response to God's gracious love. Faithful discernment should yield its fruit in actions that reflect God's character and Spirit. The parallel statements are antithetic, contrasting "everyone who loves" with "whoever is without love," hence the negative sign in unit C^{-1}.

C	4:7 Beloved, let us love one another, because love is of God; everyone who loves is begotten by God and *knows God.*	C^{-1}	4:8 Whoever is without love *does not know God*, for God is love.

From this, it becomes apparent that all spiritual discernment must be rooted in love: God's love for us first and foremost, then our sharing of that original love with one another. There is no doctrinal compartmentalization of the Christian faith: belief and spirituality cannot be understood and lived aside from the love ethic. If the spirit experienced is truly God's Spirit, it teaches God's concern for our flesh through the incarnation of the Son, and overflows in acts of love that care for other people's flesh. This is why the scholarly attempt to divide the letter in sections alternating between faith and love ultimately derails: the author's purpose is precisely to show how faith and love must go hand in hand.[5]

---

[5] The attempt was so launched by Theodor Häring, "Gedankengang und Grundgedanke des ersten Johannesbriefs," in *Theologische Abhandlungen*, ed. A. von Harnack (Mohr Siebeck, 1892). Then follow Alan E. Brooke, *A Critical and Exegetical Commentary on the Johannine Epistles* (T&T Clark, 1964); Frederick F. Bruce, *The Epistles of John* (Pickering & Inglis, 1970); Charles H. Talbert, *A Literary and Theological Commentary on the Johannine Epistles* (Crossroad, 1994); Georg Strecker, *The Johannine Letters*, trans. L. M.

Spirits at Work

The call for discernment in 1 Jn 4:1–6 appeals to the readers' acumen when readers are challenged by fresh prophecy: Is this new teaching coming from God or not? Most scholars identify the "false prophets" that "have gone out into the world" of 1 Jn 4:1c with the "antichrists" that "went out from us" in 1 Jn 2:18–19. It would be hard not to do so, since the false prophets speak with the spirit of the antichrist in 4:3bc. Also, the "false" prophets (*pseudoprophētai*) "do not acknowledge Jesus," just as the antichrists are "liars" (*pseustēs*) who deny that Jesus is the Christ, Son of the Father (1 Jn 2:22–23). The same accusations connect false prophets and antichrists, so we may confidently assume that there is only one group of dissidents throughout the letter.

The group of former members who seceded from Johannine fellowship has continued to act as a group, to confess some sort of Christian-inspired religious faith, and to make new disciples "in the world," speaking the language of the world (1 Jn 4:5). They prove to be successful in their evangelization; emboldened by their success, they obviously claim to prophesy by the power and authority of the Spirit of God. This preoccupies the author of First John, because the remainder of his flock may be shaken in their faith by the success of the dissenters. They may also be confused by the use of common Christian terms with a slant that leads into a different theology and behavior than the message that they heard from the beginning (1 Jn 1:1, 5; 3:11).

Confusion is inevitable when Christian groups or churches interpret the common heritage in different ways. All Christians

---

Mahoney, Hermeneia (Fortress, 1996); Johannes Beutler, *Die Johannesbriefe* (Verlag Friedrich Pustet, 2000); John Painter, *1, 2, and 3 John*, Sacra Pagina 18 (Liturgical, 2002).

may confess Jesus as the Christ, yet some might understand this confession of faith in *diverging* ways or construe the gospel and its demands on us in *incompatible* ways. It is one thing to hold the rich diversity of expressions of the common faith in high esteem. It is another thing altogether to undermine the common faith by an interpretation that *leads away* from it, that saps the very substance of the faith while speaking the same traditional words. Diversity and difference are to be encouraged *within* the common faith—such is the ecumenical path toward communion; *diverging* and *warring* attitudes on the other hand lead to the suspicion of falsifying the truth of the gospel and to the breakup of fellowship.

One may well ask, In what spirit are claims about God or Christ made? Are such claims made to dissolve, destroy, or dissipate efforts for fellowship and unity, out of covetousness for power and boastfulness in personal success? If so, such claims fail the ecclesiological test described earlier. They betray a mundane inclination (1 Jn 2:16). If these claims are made to *sever* the spiritual realm from the bodily one, diminishing the value or the needs of the poor or of any living being, created by God and found "good" by its Creator (Gn 1:31), then such claims fail the Christological test, also described earlier. God embraced the goodness of God's created world by sending the Son "in the flesh" (1 Jn 4:2b).[6] The Son of God lived to the full both the marvels and the limitations of incarnate being. He joined our existence in the flesh to communicate the life of God

---

[6] Commenting on Jn 1:14, Mary L. Coloe perceptively says, "In announcing that the Word became flesh (*sarx*), the divine action is not narrowed to humanity but is extended to include the entire created reality" ("Theological Reflections on Creation in the Gospel of John," *Pacifica* 24 [2011]: 11). See also Kathleen P. Rushton, "The Cosmology of John 1:1–14 and Its Implications for Ethical Action in This Ecological Age," *Colloquium* 45, no. 2 (2013): 137–53; Dorothy Lee, *Flesh and Glory: Symbolism, Gender and Theology in the Gospel of John* (Crossroad, 2002), 29–64; "Ecology and the Johannine Literature," *St. Mark's Review* 212, no. 2 (2010): 39–50.

(1 Jn 4:9). He laid down his life on the cross to save us from our hatred (1 Jn 3:15–16). Redemption is from *sin*, not from an embodied life (1 Jn 4:10).[7]

Any so-called spirituality that disengages from caring for the flesh of the poor and from caring for all flesh in the created world is a lie, a misrepresentation of the Christian faith, a false prophecy that misleads the people of God into idolatry, regardless of how it adopts the lofty language of the spiritual. First John even intuits the work of the devil behind such pretense, following the "spirit of deceit" (1 Jn 4:6c).

When faced with the facts of widespread human misery or ecological disaster, many are tempted to flee upward toward a disembodied faith in God and an eternal bliss that, in fact, negate the incarnation and disavow the laying down of Christ's life for us. Faith teaches us that there is more to this world than mere flesh and our mortal condition. However, more is not less. That is, "more" means adding the spiritual dimension, not subtracting the corporeal foundation of our existence. Some would think that charity, justice, and environmentalism are add-ons to the core of the Christian faith, that one can be a faithful Christian without them. Some Catholics would even criticize Pope Francis for having indulged in writing a full encyclical letter on such a peripheral concern to the faith as the environmental crisis: *Laudato Si'*. Hopefully, our reading of First John may provide

---

[7] Early heresies like Docetism—from the Greek verb *dokein*, "to seem"—held that Christ didn't take on human flesh exactly, only seemed or appeared to do so. To the educated mind, it was shocking to imagine the divine so crudely immersed in "the limitations of fleshliness, particularly its inevitable involvement in change, decay and suffering" (Judith M. Lieu, *I, II, & III John: A Commentary* [Westminster John Knox Press, 2008], 169). First John's insistence on Jesus coming "in the flesh" may be aimed against an incipient docetic confession of Jesus Christ by those who left the Johannine community. Raymond E. Brown, *The Epistles of John*, Anchor Bible 30 (Doubleday, 1982), 504–5, thinks the secessionist denied the salvific import of the incarnation.

some insight into the Christological anchoring of *Laudato Si'*.[8] As I've discussed, one of the key purposes of this book is to show how concern for the poor and for the environment is not peripheral but rather core to the articulation of the Christian faith in Scripture.

God's Spirit of Love

God's Spirit has been shared, given so that we might dwell in covenantal fellowship with God (1 Jn 3:24; 4:13). All living beings made of flesh partake in the covenant of life (Gn 9:8–11): we enjoy life by God's grace and abide in God's laws given to the natural world. All living beings receive a share of God's Spirit, without which we would not be alive. The Spirit of God—the Living One and the creator—gushes through all life-forms, connecting us to a thriving network: the web of life, the biosphere on Earth. We must learn to honor the Spirit of God present in all earthlings—much like ancient aboriginal cultures, albeit without worshiping created beings or natural forces. Environmental sensitivity does not necessarily imply animism or pantheism. God's Spirit is present in every one of God's creatures, yet no creature may be mistaken for God. We are surrounded by God's blessing on the living!

Unfortunately, many only see competition, predation, and violence among the living: the so-called law of the jungle, whereby in the wilderness only the strongest and fittest survive. This view of the natural order is very narrow and heavily dis-

---

[8] Pope Francis reminds us that Jesus "was far removed from philosophies which despised the body, matter and the things of the world" (*Laudato Si'*, 98). He adds, "One Person of the Trinity entered into the created cosmos, throwing in his lot with it, even to the cross. From the beginning of the world, but particularly through the incarnation, the mystery of Christ is at work in a hidden manner in the natural world as a whole, without thereby impinging on its autonomy" *(Laudato Si'*, 99).

torted, a projection of our social fears, cravings, and ambitions. Sickness, aging, predation, and death are necessary components of the circle of life on Earth, keeping populations in check, healthy and in balance. Hatred, cruelty, exploitation, violence, and genocide are altogether different. They constitute human sin, not some natural extension of the food chain. Those who would justify their abuse of power based on the natural order are false prophets, preaching under a "spirit of deceit" and only serving themselves. Humans are no more entitled to wiping out other species than to enslaving other humans or to keeping others' livelihood for themselves. We are all accountable before God for the blood we shed (Gn 9:5).

Fortunately, scientists are always discovering and documenting other forces at work in the natural world: cooperation, resilience, solidarity, self-sacrifice, care for the weak, and so on. Animals that we mistook for simple beasts show outstanding traits of behavior toward the common good. However instinctual these gestures might be, the Earth is better off with them than with any "rationally" planned evil of humans. Even trees appear to come to each others' aid through their root systems, with the collaboration of fungi networks.[9]

Human beings are endowed with a special portion of God's Spirit, having been created in God's image (Gn 1:26–27). This entails a higher call and a heavier burden than plants or animals can bear. Humans *know* of God's love for God's creatures (1 Jn 4:7–8). We are called to acknowledge divine love, to cherish it, and to spread it around generously. In human history, God has disclosed God's abundant love by sending God's Son in human

---

[9] For a couple of surprising—and scientifically documented—reads on the spirit of collaboration among animals and plants, see Peter Wohlleben, *The Hidden Life of Trees: What They Feel, How They Communicate—Discoveries from a Secret World*, trans. Jane Billinghurst (Greystone, 2016); Wohlleben, *The Inner Life of Animals: Love, Grief, and Compassion—Surprising Observations of a Hidden World*, trans. Jane Billinghurst (Greystone, 2021).

flesh (1 Jn 4:9) to reestablish love and harmony in creation after the chaos brought about by human hatred and sin (1 Jn 4:10). The only way forward is for us humans to respond to God's initiative with gratitude, faith, and fortitude. Creation awaits its redemption by means of our responsible share of God's love poured upon our hearts. We cannot falter or shirk our responsibility. We must acknowledge our place in the web of life, becoming aware of our impact on the viability of life on the planet. God's love will be "brought to perfection in us" (1 Jn 4:12) when we cease to look out only for our own petty interests and we start caring for the needs of other human beings and other living species.[10]

God's presence to creation will become visible and tangible when God's Spirit of love gushes forth from our hearts into the world, repairing what we have broken, mending our relations, and keeping up God's covenantal promise of enduring life. Love is the ultimate test of the spirits, according to First John. It is the theological test, since "God is love" (1 Jn 4:8). Love has but one source: God (1 Jn 4:7). Christian or not, whoever loves and cares for the flesh of the poor and the flesh of living beings on Earth shows to be indwelt by the Spirit of God. To paraphrase St. Paul (1 Cor 12:3), no one can love except by the Holy Spirit of God.

---

[10] For a thorough reassessment of the value of the natural world for Christian theology and ethics, see Elizabeth A. Johnson, *Ask the Beasts: Darwin and the God of Love* (Bloomsbury, 2014); Johnson, *Creation and the Cross: The Mercy of God for a Planet in Peril* (Orbis Books, 2018).

8

Witnessing to God's Love

4:14 Moreover, we have seen and testify that the Father sent his Son as savior of the world. **15** Whoever acknowledges that Jesus is the Son of God, God remains in him and he in God. **16** We have come to know and to believe in the love God has for us.

God is love, and whoever remains in love remains in God and God in him. **17** In this is love brought to perfection among us, that we have confidence on the day of judgment because as he is, so are we in this world. **18** There is no fear in love, but perfect love drives out fear because fear has to do with punishment, and so one who fears is not yet perfect in love. **19** We love because he first loved us. **20** If anyone says, "I love God," but hates his brother, he is a liar; for whoever does not love a brother whom he has seen cannot love God whom he has not seen. **21** This is the commandment we have from him: whoever loves God must also love his brother.

5:1 Everyone who believes that Jesus is the Christ is begotten by God, and everyone who loves the father loves [also] the one begotten by him. **2** In this way we know that we love the children of God when we love God and obey his commandments. **3** For the love of God is this, that we keep his commandments. And his commandments are not burdensome, **4** for whoever is begotten by God conquers the world. And the victory that conquers the world is our faith. **5** Who [indeed] is the victor over the world but the one who believes that Jesus is the Son of God?

6 This is the one who came through water and blood, Jesus Christ, not by water alone, but by water and blood. The Spirit is the one that testifies, and the Spirit is truth. **7** So there are three that testify,[1] **8** the Spirit, the water, and the blood, and the three are of one accord. **9** If we accept human testimony, the testimony of God is surely greater. Now the testimony of God is this, that he has testified on behalf of his Son. **10** Whoever believes in the Son of God has this

---

[1] The well-known King James Version (KJV) offers an expansion of the text, inserted between verses 7 and 8, that reads, "In heaven, the Father, the Word, and the Holy Ghost: and these three are one. And there are three that bear witness in earth." These words are absent from all Greek manuscripts before the fifteenth century. They are found in Latin versions of the seventh and eighth centuries. They were translated back into later Greek copies and thus made their way into the KJV. Scholars are unanimous that the so-called Johannine Comma was never part of the original letter. Given the widespread influence of the KJV, most commentaries still mention and explain the expanded text.

testimony within himself. Whoever does not believe God has made him a liar by not believing the testimony God has given about his Son.

1 Jn 4:14–5:10

In verse 4:14, the author of First John reintroduces the task of "witnessing" (*martyreō*) to what has been "seen" (*theaomai*), a combination of verbs absent since the preamble of the letter. "We have seen [*tetheametha*] and testify [*martyroumen*]" in 1 Jn 4:14 recalls the powerful opening of the letter with the words "what we have seen [*etheasametha*] with our eyes" and further, "we have seen and testify [*martyroumen*] to it," in 1 Jn 1:1–2. Such reintroduction of leading terms from the preamble signals a final turn in the spiraling argument of the letter. As the speaker makes one more round of arguments to draw in the key related issues he wants to discuss, he recapitulates the "testimony" he set out to deploy.

The vocabulary of witnessing that is reintroduced in 1 Jn 4:14 becomes prevalent in 1 Jn 5:6–11, as the multiple occurrences of the verb "testify" and the noun "testimony" show in the USCCB translation of those verses. The topic dominates the whole section of 1 Jn 4:14–5:10, however, as its contents deal with the object and the manner of the testimony. The nature of the Johannine witness to the Christian faith is set to unfold.

The Train of Thought in 4:14–5:10

The beginning and end of the section set in parallel the testimony of the Johannine fellowship with the very testimony of God. Both testimonies relate to the sending or coming of the Son of God and the salvation found in him. The following table shows the relevant recurring vocabulary that supports the parallelism.

A (4:14-16)	A' (5:6-10)
We . . . testify	The one that testifies Three that testify Human testimony The testimony of God He has testified The testimony God has given
The Father sent his *Son* As savior of the world	This is the one who came through water and blood, *Jesus Christ*
Whoever acknowledges that Jesus is the Son of God We have come to know and to believe in the love God *has* for [lit. "in"] us	Whoever believes / the one who believes in the Son of God / that Jesus is the Son of God Whoever does not believe / by not believing *Has* this testimony *within* himself

Noticing the parallelism helps to provide a way to solve some of the intriguing exegetical issues in these verses. For instance, scholars wonder whether God's testimony in 5:9–10 is distinct[2] or equal[3] to the testimony given by spirit, water, and blood in 5:6–8. If the parallelism holds, then the testimony given by

---

[2] So think Rudolf Schnackenburg, *The Johannine Epistles* (Crossroad, 1992), 238–39; Raymond E. Brown, *The Epistles of John*, Anchor Bible 30 (Doubleday, 1982), 586–87; John Painter, *1, 2, and 3 John*, Sacra Pagina 18 (Liturgical, 2002), 309.

[3] So think James L. Houlden, *A Commentary on the Johannine Epistles* (Adam & Charles Black, 1973), 132; Ian H. Marshall, *The Epistles of John* (Eerdmans, 1978), 239–40; Stephen S. Smalley, *1, 2, 3 John* (Word, 1984), 283–84; Daniel L. Akin, *1, 2, 3 John* (B&H, 2001), 200; Kelly Anderson and Daniel Keating, *James, First, Second, and Third John*, Catholic Commentary on Sacred Scripture (Baker Academic, 2017), 232.

spirit, water, and blood *is* God's testimony, mediated through these elements.

Another puzzle is whether the three elements (spirit, water, blood) refer in some way to the incarnation or death of Christ, to the salvation he brought, or to the remembrance of his coming or death and the reception of salvation in the sacraments of the church—namely baptism and the Eucharist.[4] The parallelism of verse 5:6 with verse 4:14 would advocate for a both/and approach to this complex question, since verse 4:14 is both a Christological and a soteriological statement; that is, it focuses as much on the Son of God coming in the flesh as it does on his role as savior.

The middle of the section is split in two units that run parallel to each other: verses 4:17–21 (unit B) and verses 5:1–5 (unit B′). The former (unit B) develops the love ethic, from its origin in God ("he first loved us," 4:19) to its completion and fruitfulness in our own bold acts of love for others ("perfect love" and "confidence," 4:17–18). The latter (unit B′) suggests that such boldness and confidence in love come from our faith, which empowers us to be victorious over the world's mundane coveting and hatred of the poor. Both units are connected by the core argument that whoever pretends to love God must also show love to God's children. The following table sketches the verbal parallels that connect the units.

---

[4] For a clear and succinct presentation of the different lines of interpretation, see Duane F. Watson, *The Letters of John* (Cambridge University Press, 2024), 138–41. Full discussion in Brown, *The Epistles of John*, 573–85. The very existence of the Johannine Comma (see note 1 in this chapter) shows a medieval attempt at interpretation.

B (4:17-21)	B' (5:1-5)
This is the *commandment* we have from him:	Obey his *commandments* Keep his *commandments* His *commandments* are not burdensome.
Whoever loves God must also love his *brother*. Whoever does not love a *brother* whom he has seen cannot love God whom he has not seen.	Everyone who loves the father loves [also] the one begotten by him.
As he [Jesus] is, so are we in this *world*.	Whoever is begotten by God conquers the *world*.

Commentators usually remark on a shift from the topic of love in 4:7–21 to the topic of faith in chapter 5. However, since 5:1–3 still mention love—and faith, together—interpreters sometimes wait until 5:4 or 5:5 to indicate the start of a new section.[5] This forces First John into a straitjacket of clean topic borders, which actually breaks apart the message the author is specifically trying to convey: "We have come to know and *to believe in the love God has for us*" (4:16a). Our faith is in God's love for us. There is no point in attempting to separate the topic of faith from the topic of love. Such separation betrays Johannine theology by imposing our clean—and lifeless—Cartesian thinking.

The Johannine confession of *faith* is that Jesus is the Son of God sent for our salvation (Jn 3:16–17; 1 Jn 4:14). To acknowledge that Jesus is the Son of God (4:15a), to believe that Jesus is the Christ (5:1), to believe that Jesus is the Son of God (5:5b), to believe in the Son of God (5:10a) . . . is to confess his *coming* in "water" and "blood" (5:6), in the very messiness of the flesh of Jesus of Nazareth, who laid down his personal life out of love

---

[5] See chapter 7, note 2, for examples from published scholars.

for us (3:16), who bled to his death for all of us. How can we not love God's children and God's creatures after that? After being *so* loved by God? To truly believe in who Jesus is, to be saved in such faith, means to channel such life and love unto others—life and love poured in our hearts and overflowing from our hearts.

In fact, given First John's insistence on the inextricable connection between faith and love,[6] most likely it was the key point of contention with those who departed from the fellowship (2:18–19; 4:1). Surely, in their ongoing mission "in the world" (4:3–5), they spoke of faith and of love, from the word received by all Johannine brethren from the beginning (1:5; 3:11). Nevertheless, the author accuses them of denying Christ (2:22–23) and maybe of loving only in words, not in true deeds (3:18). He seems to argue against a faulty understanding of Christ as coming "by water alone," insisting he came "by water and blood" (5:6b). In Johannine parlance, this might actually mean that the Son of God did not fully come among us until he actually bled his last drop of blood on the cross for us. God lovingly met with God's creatures, espousing misery, plight, and death through the suffering, in the flesh, of Jesus the Just. The solemn witness of the Beloved Disciple in the Fourth Gospel could be thus explained (Jn 19:34–35). To deny the blood would amount in his eyes to deny the incarnation altogether (1 Jn 4:2–3), as the "spirit of deceit" might incite some to prophesy (4:6).

Quite possibly the only wrongdoing exemplified in the letter—refusing responsibility and compassion for those in material need (3:17)—was the ethical outcome of a faith that agreed on high praise for Christ's words but paid little or no attention to the way in which he led his life to the bitter end. If Jesus were God's Son, he could not have meant to die on a Roman cross;

---

[6] On this particular topic, see Garrett C. Kenney, *The Relation of Christology to Ethics in the First Epistle of John* (University Press of America, 2000), esp. 45–46, 49.

that piece of his life would have been irrelevant or denied by the dissenters. To partake in poverty, to share in the fate of the poor, requires a faith that sees Christ among the poor. To love in the sweet comfort of words only betrays a faith that places Christ high and away from the poor—a "spirit" of "false prophecy," which actually knows nothing of God (4:8).

Water, Spirit, Blood

All living earthlings require water and bodily fluids—most require oxygen, too—and all that live above water take their oxygen from the air, another gaseous fluid. The chemistry of life is facilitated by the constant exchange of its building blocks carried by fluids. Life started in water and carried on outside of water, provided that some water was available, both in the soil and in the air. Desiccated bodies are dead organisms. All life-forms are connected through the water cycle and the currents—liquid and gaseous—of the biosphere. No wonder that water, spirit, and blood became religious symbols of life; nobody is alive without them.

In the Fourth Gospel, water that flows ("living" water) is promised to quench the thirst of the Samaritan woman (Jn 4:10, 13–15) and of anyone else who believes in Jesus (Jn 7:37–39). In both cases, the flow of water turns into the flow of Spirit, providing life:

> Everyone who drinks this *water* will be thirsty again; but whoever drinks the *water* I shall give will never thirst; the *water* I shall give will become in him a spring of *water* welling up to *eternal life*. (Jn 4:13b–14)
>
> But the hour is coming, and is now here, when true worshipers will worship the Father in *Spirit* and truth; and indeed the Father seeks such people to worship him.

> God is *Spirit*, and those who worship him must worship in *Spirit* and truth. (Jn 4:23–24)
>
> On the last and greatest day of the feast, Jesus stood up and exclaimed, "Let anyone who thirsts come to me and drink. Whoever believes in me, as scripture says: 'Rivers of *living water* will flow from within him.'" (Jn 7:37–38)
>
> He said this in reference to the *Spirit* that those who came to believe in him were to receive. There was, of course, no *Spirit* yet, because Jesus had not yet been glorified. (Jn 7:39).

It is widely recognized that the hour of Jesus's glorification in John is the hour of his passion and death, when he is "lifted up" on the cross (Jn 3:14–15; 12:31–33). From up on the cross, Jesus expires, giving away the *Spirit* (Jn 19:30). *Water* and *blood* also flow out from his side, pierced by a soldier's lance (Jn 19:34). That Jesus is providing his very own bodily fluids for believers to consume—however symbolically—is also clear from the call to drink his blood and eat his flesh in the bread-of-life discourse:

> Whoever eats my flesh and drinks my blood has eternal life, and I will raise him on the last day. For my flesh is true food, and my blood is true drink. Whoever eats my flesh and drinks my blood remains in me and I in him. Just as the living Father sent me and I have life because of the Father, so also the one who feeds on me will have life because of me. (Jn 6:54–57)

The mystery of divine life being communicated to mortal beings like us is expressed in tangible and—however shocking—*biological* ways: flesh to eat, blood and water to drink, air to breathe. The church mediates this religious experience of divine indwelling through the sacraments, most eminently so in the

Eucharist, using wine and bread as nutrients. While Christians readily recognize the historical connection to Jesus's Last Supper, we fail to recognize the biological foundation for meaning. Just as the historical figure of the Beloved Disciple testified to Jesus laying down his life for us (Jn 19:35; 1 Jn 3:16), so do the natural elements testify to the truth of divine life being offered in flesh, water, blood, and spirit:

> So there are three that testify, the *Spirit*, the *water*, and the *blood*, and the three are of one accord. If we accept human testimony, the testimony of God is surely greater. Now the testimony of God is this, that he has testified on behalf of his Son. (1 Jn 5:7–9)
> This is how you can know the *Spirit* of God: every *spirit* that acknowledges Jesus Christ *come in the flesh* belongs to God, and every *spirit* that does not acknowledge Jesus does not belong to God. (1 Jn 4:2–3a)

Nature and history both reveal the One True God and the divine gift of enduring life. Just as we need bodily fluids to survive and thrive as flesh-and-blood human beings, so do we need the water, the blood, and the Spirit that God can provide to be in fellowship with one another and with God. These were offered once and for all (history) in and by the Son of God, who delivered himself that we might live in him and through him. God's gifts bring life to us, and it is fitting to our senses and to our earthly minds that they be fluids in language and appearance (nature).

Desecrating the Earth by polluting its oceans, rivers, lakes, and fountains; by warming up and toxifying the air we breathe; by denying access to clean water and air to the poor makes God a liar (1 Jn 5:10), a giver of ill gifts. To normalize the extensive disfiguring of nature as inconsequential is to portray God as the Creator of corruption and evil. No complicit silence may stand for acquittal. The water spoiled, the blood of the poor spilled, and the toxic fumes we emit testify against us that we have brought about death—just as the pure water, the precious blood, and the holy Spirit handed over by Jesus on our behalf testify to God's good will for us to live.

Faith in God's Love

The state of the world and the plight of the poor, when taken seriously, may bring any lucid mind to the verge of despair. A humanitarian crisis somewhere, a bloody conflict over territory and resources, or a natural disaster elsewhere might be occasional blows we can take in and absorb, our faith still standing. The challenge is to witness so much wrongdoing happening almost everywhere and at all times, from family feuds up close to the leveling of cities by missiles happening far away. In Jesus's time—a cynical person would argue—it was easier to love thy neighbor because there were so few of them! For one thing, we were nowhere near the billion population that we reached in 1800, a number that we have multiplied by eight in under three centuries. For another, we were so spread out that our meager means of transportation and communication meant that populations had very little or slow impact on each other.

Nowadays, our screens bring us live news from everywhere simultaneously, and the global market setup means resources are up for grabs even from afar, making us all the more prone to conflict and dispute with people we have not even met. Everyone becomes my neighbor, and every neighbor's plight has a claim on my conscience. So much suffering and hatred can be overwhelming for the human heart.

As the Twenty-Ninth Conference of the Parties (COP 29) to the UN Framework on Climate Change met in Azerbaijan in November 2024, previously colonized, poor, and vulnerable countries pleaded for financial help from well-developed former colonial countries that grew rich on their resources.[7] This financial help is essential to back the necessary world transition to renewable energies, in order to lower fossil-fuel emissions that will tip the world over the 1.5 degree Celsius (2.7 degrees Fahrenheit) average temperature increase. As of now, current pledges—if implemented—set us up for disaster, with an average temperature increase of 3.2 Celsius (5.8 Fahrenheit) by the end of the twenty-first century. This generation of eight billion people is thus facing the challenge of changing its lifestyle throughout the world in less than thirty years.

Most poignantly, richer countries are challenged to share their livelihood with poorer ones, so that all can make the necessary changes. Can humanity rise to the challenge together? If humans do not learn to let go of their privileges and love each other soon enough, deep enough in their pockets, "in deed and truth" (1 Jn 3:18), this time around all creation will suffer the consequences—literally.

It would seem that the prophet Daniel's words never rang truer: "It shall be a time unsurpassed in distress since nations began until that time" (Dan 12:1). Daniel, of course, was reflecting on the distress lived by the people of Israel in his own time and place, more than a century before Christ, under foreign Greek rule. Jews were being forced to assimilate to the dominant Greek culture, threatened with torture and death unless they abandoned their allegiance to God and the covenant. One can imagine Daniel's disarray. Every generation has witnessed its own share of horror stories. (Imagine Daniel's dismay if he had been a witness to the Shoah.) Rachel's lament over her lost children, too, would never have rung truer than then (Jer 31:15; Mt 2:18).

---

[7] United Nations, Climate Action, "COP29 Concludes with Climate Finance Deal," accessed November 19, 2024, un.org.

The question is this: How do we keep faith and hope alive in the midst of evil and chaos unleashed, when there seems no reason to love or forgive?

One might even conclude that there is not, that there could not ever be, enough love in the world to wipe away so many tears, to heal so many deep wounds.

When faced with utter destruction, with overwhelming pain everywhere, and no willingness to compromise from any side of a conflict, of what use are the tenets of Christian belief?

I wish I could convey a ready-to-use theological answer to all predicaments, a verse we might pull out of our Bible and plaster all wounds with it. None of that sort exists. Yet I too must bear witness to First John's insight on these poignant questions, and so I humbly and very quietly forward the following.

Out of respect for real flesh-and-blood suffering and mourning, I wish I could end this chapter here, in silence. But there is nowhere near enough love around to help grieve and heal the fathoms of suffering of the poor, the abused, and the oppressed. We could never love enough. We would drown in a sea of tears. Ours is not the source of love, but God's.

> In this is love: not that we have loved God, but that he loved us and sent his Son as expiation for our sins. (1 Jn 4:10)

We have not even been able to truly love God, who has done no wrong to us, never mind our fellow human beings or the rest of creation for that matter. Nonetheless, God has loved us, forgiven us, and sent us God's very precious Son that we may be healed by God's love and live.

In the very dying of Jesus Christ on the cross, in the sharing of his Spirit, water, and blood to the very last drop, God has reached out and joined us in our wounded flesh, opening a way for us to know true love and to begin to love.

> Beloved, if God so loved us, we also must love one another. No one has ever seen God. Yet, if we love one another, God remains in us, and his love is brought to perfection in us. (1 Jn 4:11–12)

True love heals, transforms, and empowers. It energizes and pours out like water, blood, and spirit. Like those life-sustaining fluids, love begets life, sustains life, and makes life grow and flourish. Love regenerates. Whoever has been loved has been born anew, from God, who is love:

> Beloved, let us love one another, because love is of God; everyone who loves is begotten by God and knows God. Whoever is without love does not know God, for God is love. (1 Jn 4:7–8)

And so the tenets of the Christian faith do matter in the end. First John argues that to believe in Jesus Christ is to believe in God sending God's Son in the flesh to pour out God's love, life, and forgiveness unto us, and to transform us into new creatures capable of loving others in turn. Johannine Christology is not an abstract endeavor, disconnected from human and earthly conditions. It is no mere fancy intellectual prowess or a list of lofty divine titles for Jesus of Nazareth. It is the joyful message of salvation that frees us from our conditioned and sterile thinking that there is no solution to our plight: "The truth will set you free" (Jn 8:32b).

The only way out of this worldly mess of coveting, indifference, and hatred is to believe in the transforming power of God's love for us. The force that conquers the logic of world dominance is actually faith.

> For whoever is begotten by God conquers the world. And the victory that conquers the world is our faith. (1 Jn 5:4).

Nor is it just any faith, but faith in the transforming power of God's love for us:

> We have come to know and to believe in the love God has for us. God is love, and whoever remains in love remains in God and God in him. (1 Jn 4:16)

Doubt, despair, fear, and anxiety paralyze. We freeze before the immensity and the complexity of the problems before us. We lock ourselves in and shut the others out. We blame instead of forgiving, instead of giving forward. We give up when we are called to be bold before God's judgment and to take the first steps, steps that God will bring to fruition and to "perfection" in God's own time.

> In this is love brought to perfection among us, that we have confidence on the day of judgment because as he is, so are we in this world. There is no fear in love, but perfect love drives out fear because fear has to do with punishment, and so one who fears is not yet perfect in love. We love because he first loved us. (1 Jn 4:17–19)

The key to bold and steady, perseverant, Christian commitment toward the poor and toward our choking planet is our faith. Only by contemplating God's love for us, pouring out from Jesus's pierced side on the cross,[8] shall we find the inspiration, the overflow of *life*, the strength, the courage, the solidarity, and the love to act as needed—tuning down our *lifestyle* for the sake of the Earth, sharing our *livelihood* with the poor for the *life* of the world, now.

---

[8] On the riches flowing from Jesus's open heart, see Pope Francis's 2024 encyclical letter, *Dilexit nos*, esp. chapters 4 and 5. First John is cited in nos. 167–71. On the flow of water, blood, and spirit, see nos. 92–101.

9

Embracing the Fellowship of Life

❦

5:11 And this is the testimony: God gave us eternal life, and this life is in his Son. **12** Whoever possesses the Son has life; whoever does not possess the Son of God does not have life.

13 I write these things to you so that you may know that you have eternal life, you who believe in the name of the Son of God. **14** And we have this confidence in him, that if we ask anything according to his will, he hears us. **15** And if we know that he hears us in regard to whatever we ask, we know that what we have asked him for is ours. **16** If anyone sees his brother sinning, if the sin is not deadly, he should pray to God and he will give him life. This is only for those whose sin is not deadly. There is such a thing as deadly sin, about which I do not say that you should pray. **17** All wrongdoing is sin, but there is sin that is not deadly.

18 We know that no one begotten by God sins; but the one begotten by God he protects, and the evil one cannot touch him. **19** We know that we belong to God, and the whole world is under the power of the evil one. **20** We also know that the Son of God has come and has given us discernment to know the one who is true. And we are in the one who is true, in his Son Jesus Christ. He is the true God and eternal life. **21** Children, be on your guard against idols.

1 Jn 5:11–21

Verse 5:13 closely recalls the conclusion to the Fourth Gospel in Jn 20:31. In both cases, the purpose of the writing is stated, and it has to do with obtaining life through faith in Jesus as the Son of God. For readers of the Fourth Gospel, the writing sustains faith, whereas it provides assurance to the readers of First John.

But these [signs] are written that you may [come to] believe that Jesus is the Messiah, the Son of God, and that through this belief you may have life in his name. (Jn 20:31)
I write these things to you so that you may know that you have eternal life, you who believe in the name of the Son of God. (1 Jn 5:13)

This close resemblance has prompted many commentators to take 1 Jn 5:13–21 as the conclusion of the letter.[1] Others view 5:13

---

[1] Rudolf Schnackenburg, *The Johannine Epistles* (Crossroad, 1992), 238–39; Raymond E. Brown, *The Epistles of John*, Anchor Bible 30 (Doubleday, 1982), 630–33; John Painter, *1, 2, and 3 John*, Sacra Pagina 18 (Liturgical, 2002), 312–15; George Parsenios, *First, Second, and Third John* (Baker, 2014), 124–29; Kelly Anderson and Daniel Keating, *James, First, Second, and Third John*, Catholic Commentary on Sacred Scripture (Baker Academic,

as the final verse concluding the preceding section, leaving out verses 5:14–21 as some sort of an epilogue, just like Jn 21 does for the Fourth Gospel, which ends in Jn 20:31.[2] Either way, the close parallel to the Gospel blurs perception of the letter's own distinctive markings. In this case, it is important to note a formal *inclusio* between 1 Jn 5:11 and 5:20. In both verses, "eternal life" is to be found in the Son of God, Jesus Christ. This is the main topic of the last section of the letter (1 Jn 5:11–21) and rightfully so, since it also beautifully rounds off a letter that started with the manifestation of "eternal life" in the Son (1 Jn 1:1–2).

This last section serves as a recapitulation of main points of the letter. Foremost, it notes that a right understanding of Jesus Christ opens up the divine riches flowing from fellowship with the true God (5:20), as opposed to the misleading stance of idolatrous teaching (5:21) that is so popular in our world (5:19).

The Train of Thought in 5:11–21

Verse 5:11 smoothly transitions from the topic of testimony of the previous section (4:14–5:10) to the topic of eternal life in this final section of the letter. God's testimony on behalf of Jesus was alluded to in 5:10. Now God's testimony is shown to be that God's most precious gift—eternal or enduring life—is borne by the Son of God, who has been sent "in the flesh" into the world. To welcome this Son with faith is to receive the enduring life he brings to share with us (5:11–12).

2017), 234–42; Duane F. Watson, *The Letters of John* (Cambridge University Press, 2024), 141–51.

[2] Edward Malatesta, *Interiority and Covenant: A Study of εἶναι ἐν and μένειν ἐν in the First Letter of Saint John* (Biblical Institute, 1978), 318–20; Stephen S. Smalley, *1, 2, 3 John* (Word, 1984), 292–94; Johannes Beutler, *Die Johannesbriefe* (Verlag Friedrich Pustet, 2000), 127–28; Michelle Morgen, *Les épîtres de Jean*, Commentaire biblique: Nouveau Testament 19 (Cerf, 2005), 200–203; Judith M. Lieu, *I, II, & III John: A Commentary* (Westminster John Knox, 2008), 220–22.

The community that has placed its trust in a crucified Jesus need not fear to have come short of the precious gift of enduring life. The author's purpose is to reassure them (5:13) that no further teaching is needed (2:27), no new prophecy lies out of their grasp (4:1), no spirit may resist their own judgment (4:1–6), and no special knowledge of God can be claimed (2:4) other than Jesus's example of true love through the laying down of his life (3:16). The gift of enduring life has been bequeathed unto them in the fullest revelation of how much God has loved them (3:1; 4:8–10, 16).

At the beginning of the section, verses 5:11–13 (unit A) establish this assurance. At the end of it, verses 5:18–21 (unit A′) reinforce this assurance by providing contrast with the worldly, mundane powers that impersonate and search to supplant the one true God (5:19, 21). The community of readers, or the faithful audience, is once again told that they have been given "intelligence" or "discernment" (*dianoian*, 5:20b) by the Son of God: they will not be fooled or led astray (2:26; 3:7a; 4:6c) if they keep the Word received from the beginning (1:1, 5; 2:5, 24; 3:11). This table highlights the verbal parallels between both units:

A (5:11–13)	A′ (5:18–21)
So that you may know	Discernment to know
	We know that
Eternal life, life	Eternal life
Is in his Son	*Is under* the power of the evil one
The Son	And *we are . . . in his Son*
The Son of God	The Son of God
God gave us	The Son of God . . . has given us . . . the true God

Embracing the Fellowship of Life

Reassurance provides confidence, and what better confidence before God than to intercede for others through our prayers? This is the topic at the center of the section. Verses 5:14–15 (unit B) ground the confidence of prayer in asking according to God's will. Verses 5:16–17 (unit B′) extend the assurance of salvation to others through the gift of prayer. Note the recurring vocabulary.

B (5:14–15)	B′ (5:16–17)
If we ask anything Whatever we ask What we have asked	If anyone sees . . . he should pray (ask) That you should pray (ask)

The restriction to pray only for God's forgiveness of "nondeadly sins" may strike us as odd or even uncharitable. However, strictly speaking, First John does not forbid anyone from praying for the forgiveness of the deadly sins of others.[3] The author is rather intent on praying for the nondeadly sins of brothers and sisters within the community. He seems to assume that no member of the community would commit a deadly sin (5:18), whatever that may be,[4] so the prayer of intercession is aimed at

---

[3] This position is well defended, based on the grammar of the sentence, by James B. Prothro, *The Bible and Reconciliation: Confession, Repentance, and Restoration, A Catholic Biblical Commentary on the Sacraments* (Baker Academic, 2023), 200.

[4] One should not read back into First John the later distinction between mortal and venial sin, with all its developed nuances, as they appear in the *Catechism of the Catholic Church*, paragraphs 1854–64. Notably, however, paragraph 1854 does quote this biblical passage as support for the ulterior development of tradition. Following Brown, *The Epistles of John*, 612–19, many scholars understand the "sin unto death" (*hamartia pros thanaton*) in 1 Jn 5:16–17 as the breakup of the fellowship, out of lack of charity and thus denial of the saving death of Jesus Christ. Those who leave the fellowship are antichrists (2:18–19, 22) against Christ "in the flesh" (1 Jn 4:2–3), and their disregard for the brethren in need amounts to murder (3:14–17). By embracing the values of the world (2:15–16; 4:4–5) they lie under the grasp of the evil

reinforcing fellowship among those who have already passed from death to life (3:14–15) but who may still occasionally stumble (5:16–17). In this way, any qualms regarding the assurance of salvation may be put to rest *within* the community. Such a reading is consistent with the overall goal of the final section of the letter: reassurance of the audience.

The Mirage of Idolatry: Living the Good Life

The letter comes to a close rather abruptly, with a dire warning: "Children, keep yourselves from idols" (1 Jn 5:21, translation mine). A few scholars would argue that this is a *literal* reference to the pagan gods and to the widely common polytheistic worship that surrounded the church of the early centuries.[5] Such a reading would underscore the frailty of the nascent Christian faith, immersed in a Gentile world, set apart from long-standing Jewish monotheism, and constantly assailed by social pressure to conform to imperial standards for civic worship and practice. Although totally within the broad socioreligious context, the warning would be but an afterthought hanging where it stands,

---

one (5:19), in the abode of hatred and death (3:13–15). Of themselves, they have withdrawn from divine fellowship (1:3) and forsaken the intercession of Jesus the Just (2:1), refusing to join in prayer with their former brothers and sisters (5:16–17).

[5] So think M. J. Edwards, "Martyrdom in the First Epistle of John," *Novum Testamentun* 31, no. 2 (1989): 164–71; Julian Hills, "'Little Children, Keep Yourselves from Idols': 1 Jn 5:21 Reconsidered," *Catholic Biblical Quarterly* 51, no. 2 (1989): 285–310; Hans-Joseph Klauck, *Der erste Johannesbrief* (Benzinger, 1991), 341–44; Robert W. Yarbrough, *1–3 John* (Baker Academic, 2008), 322–35. In a full-volume treatment of the verse, Terry Griffith sets First John in an early Jewish context, where the polemic against idolatry sits more naturally: *Keep Yourselves from Idols: A New Look at 1 John*, Journal for the Study of the New Testament Supplement Series 233 (Sheffield Academic, 2002).

by itself, left unpacked. There is not a hint of an issue there, in the preceding 104 verses.

The majority of interpreters suspect a *figurative* reference to some form of misrepresentation of God, Christ, and the path to everlasting life, object of the letter proper.[6] Just as there are antichrists (2:18–19), false prophets (4:1), and a spirit of deceit (4:6), there are also idols (5:21) that would take the place of "the one who is true," "the true God and eternal life" (5:20). Given the immediate context of the language in the preceding verse, this line of interpretation is highly plausible. First John ends with a challenge for the children of God to unmask all misleading impostures of the faith—notably, the obvious one carried by former members of the community now preaching to an enchanted world (4:5) a disembodied Christ (4:2–3) and spreading a lie of a love that does not take the plight of the poor seriously (3:17–18).

Taking our lead from verse 5:19b, where it is said that "the whole world is under the power of the evil one," idolatry in 5:21 becomes a charge against those who align themselves with the anti-values of the world, coveting power and riches, and boasting a livelihood (2:16–17) while not really caring for the misfortunes of the poor (3:17–18). "Might is right" could never honor the good news preached by Jesus of Nazareth, who died hanging from a cross raised by the mighty Roman empire.[7] Nonetheless, a crude misrepresentation of God's blessings ends up yielding the so-called prosperity gospel, whereby prosperity is read as a

---

[6] To list but a few, Brown, *The Epistles of John*, 627–29; Smalley, *1, 2, 3 John*, 309–10; Painter, *1, 2, and 3 John*, 328–30; Parsenios, *First, Second, and Third John*, 125–26; Anderson and Keating, *James, First, Second, and Third John*, 242; Watson, *The Letters of John*, 148–49. Lieu, *I, II, & III John*, 237, insightfully associates the idols of 1 Jn 5:21 with the world of desire and arrogance portrayed in 1 Jn 2:16.

[7] For an incisive critique of the sheer misrepresentation of Christianity in American politics, see Andrew L. Whitehead, *American Idolatry: How Christian Nationalism Betrays the Gospel and Threatens the Church* (Brazos, 2023).

simplistic sign of fidelity to God's plan. Prosperity can be quickly and easily achieved, however, by being opportunistic and ruthless while disregarding the suffering of those abused to move upward in an unjust world of unregulated competition (*anomia*, 3:4). How could such prosperity be a sign of God's blessing? It sounds much more like the prosperity of Pharaoh, built upon the crushing of the Hebrew people (Ex 1:8–14). Prosperity of this kind is an imposture of God's blessing, an idolatry.

Idolatry is appealing because it is a lure for, a glittering mirage of, and an easy way out of the Christian path of compassion and solidarity with the poor and the oppressed. No one sets out saying to oneself, *I want to become idolatrous*. Rather, we are captivated by success stories, dazed by the possibilities that success would open up, enthused maybe by how we could put all that fresh raw power to work on behalf of our loved ones. *Imagine all the good you could do*, whispers the innocent little voice in our head. We might even persuade ourselves that our success is an opportunity for the betterment of the poor and of the Earth.[8]

In the same way, the dissenters who departed from the Johannine fellowship were not eager to betray or deny Christ (1 Jn 2:22–23). They thought of themselves as being blameless, sinless (2:7, 10). They were convinced that the world finally listened to them because they got the gospel right (4:5). They thought they were inspired by the spirit of truth, knew Christ better, and so knew God (2:4). They simply moved away from the crude idea that the Son of God could bleed to death on a Roman cross (5:6), or that Jesus's death had any impact on their lives of faith (2:2;

---

[8] For a critique of how ideologies incompatible with the Christian faith can actually infiltrate our minds and bend the gospel to meet worldly standards or trends, see Pope Francis's 2018 apostolic exhortation *Gaudete et exsultate*, nos. 35–62. "In our times too, many Christians, perhaps without realizing it, can be seduced by these deceptive ideas, which reflect an anthropocentric immanentism disguised as Catholic truth" (no. 35).

4:10), or that divine love had to be confused with care for the material living conditions of people on Earth (3:17–18). They probably thought of themselves as being spiritual people, driven to contemplate and say higher things (4:1). They likely said they loved God (4:20), loved their brothers and sisters (3:14), and loved the world (2:15).

Saying is easy; doing is harder. First John challenges false pretenses and deems them evil. If we think we are completely innocent, we deceive ourselves (1:8). We should rather acknowledge our failed attempts (1:9) and rectify our commitments (3:3). To shy away from the cross is to deny Jesus, Lord of the poor (2:22). To shut our eyes from seeing the poor and to shut our guts from being moved by their plight is to love only "in word or speech," not "in deed and truth" (3:17–18). To say we love God while we abandon God's children and God's creatures to their fate is a lie (4:20). Even worse, to look away from the billion crosses that are raised in the world to ensure our comfort and peace of mind is to make God a liar (1:10; 5:10), who revealed God's love in both water and blood flowing from Jesus's side on the cross (5:6–9). If we make God a liar, it is because we have our eyes set on false gods that utter false promises of life as we indulge in our coveting and bow to the lawlessness of the world's market. If we believe the market is fair, and we aim at living the good life that the world promises, we have forsaken the gospel and yielded to nothing less than idolatry.

You might think this is hard to read; it is actually hard for me to write. Who in the world can escape the "ruler of this world" (Jn 12:31; 1 Jn 5:19b)? We are all complicit to a certain extent in the way things are run in the world (2:16). We all purchase others' work and sell ours to earn a livelihood. We can hardly escape the marketplace. To stand against the global market in solidarity with the poor is, in a sense, to stand against ourselves and to endorse our own indictment. Alternative ways of living are resisted, mocked, ostracized, and sometimes punished.

Nobody said bearing a cross would be easy.[9] It is heavy lifting. Yet, against the lies of the powerful that would keep everything as is, to their advantage, we are called to find or create new ways of dealing with others that do the least harm possible to the poor and to Earth.[10]

The all-important first step remains quite simple: Do not believe in a lie, "let no one deceive you" (3:7), do not fall in love with the trendy "things of the world" (2:15), "keep yourselves from idols" (5:21).[11]

What We Do Know

Even as idolatry blurs the world's vision of truth, faith handed over by the apostolic tradition of witnesses guides us in perceiving reality under God's light, shining forth in Christ. First John concludes with a few summary statements introduced as what "we know" (5:15, 18, 19, 20).

> We know that what we have asked him for is ours. (1 Jn 5:15b)

Assurance and boldness before God are topics treated earlier in the letter (2:28–3:3; 3:19–22; 4:17–18). In our pettiness, we

---

[9] Jesus actually said, "Whoever wishes to come after me must deny himself, take up his cross, and follow me" (Mk 8:34; Mt 16:24; Lk 14:27).

[10] For an inspiring read on this challenging and difficult topic, see Joe Blosser, *To Love Our Neighbors: Radical Practices in Solidarity, Sufficiency & Sustainability* (Orbis Books, 2024). For an example of how the monastic Rule of St. Benedict broke with the cultural, socioeconomic, and Earth-plundering values of the Roman world, see Samuel Torvend, *Monastic Ecological Wisdom: A Living Tradition* (Liturgical, 2023).

[11] Pope Benedict XVI wrote beautiful and perceptive pages on the necessity for truth to guide our charity in his 2009 encyclical, *Caritas in veritate*. "To defend the truth, to articulate it with humility and conviction, and to bear witness to it in life are therefore exacting and indispensable forms of charity" (no. 1).

tend to read this as comfort for our many individual petitions in prayer, that they will be heard and granted if according to God's will. First John has a wider, holier, and wholesome scope for this assurance. What really matters is God's blessings of life (2:25), divine begetting (3:1–3), and forgiveness for our shortcomings and sinfulness (2:1–2; 3:19–22; 5:16–17). These are the most fundamental petitions addressed by the fellowship together in prayer. These are the most fundamental gifts that we should rejoice together in receiving. The good news that they have been granted by a loving God should be of great comfort to us, for God did no less than send God's only Son to provide them in his very dying on our behalf.

> We know that no one begotten by God sins; but the one begotten by God he protects, and the evil one cannot touch him. (1 Jn 5:18)

Throughout the letter, the author has been at pains to underscore the incompatibility of darkness, sin, hatred, and negligence of our brothers' and sisters' welfare with the dignity and blessing of becoming God's children, or with claims to be spiritual and to know and love God. No true spiritual life may disengage from care for the poor and for God's beloved creatures. The grammar of the second sentence in this verse is obscured by ambiguous reference: who protects (or keeps) whom? "The one begotten by God" could refer to Christ or to any of us, now made God's children (2:29–3:3). Either God or Christ could do the "protecting," one way to translate the Greek verb *tēreō*, as in "keep safe." In this sense, God or Christ would keep believers safe from the evil one. This is what the NABRE translation implies. However, the first sentence in 5:18a clearly uses "no one begotten by God" to refer to us, believers and children of God. It would be odd to shift gears and suddenly make "the one begotten by God" in 5:18b refer to Christ. Alternatively, if both uses of the verb *gennaō* (to beget) refer to us, then we may translate the verb *tēreō* simply as "to keep," which is the way it has been translated throughout the letter, as in "keeping his commandments" (2:3–4; 3:22, 24; 5:3) or "keeping his word" (2:5). An alternative translation of the verse would thus be,

> We know that no one begotten by God sins; but the one begotten by God keeps him [God], and the evil one cannot touch him. (1 Jn 5:18, translation mine)

There is no fully convincing solution to translate 5:18b, because now we have the strange statement that, as the children of God, we keep God by not sinning, and, by keeping God, we are safe from the evil one. I still find this translation more compelling, because (a) it keeps consistent references; (b) it makes sense to "keep God" in 5:18b and to "keep" from idols in 5:21;[12] and (c) it is consistent with my translation of 3:9b: "a child of God remains in God" (see chapter 5 of this book). In my humble view, First John does not provide some magical safeguard against sin—be it a divine "seed" in us (3:9b, NABRE) or the Son of God protecting us. The only way to keep away from sin and evil is to keep close to God by doing God's will, by walking like Jesus under God's light (1:7; 2:6).

> We know that we belong to God, and the whole world is under the power of the evil one. (1 Jn 5:19)

This is as much a comfort (5:19a) as a stern warning (5:19b). Despite the dualistic antithesis, this statement is not an invita-

---

[12] Although the synonymous Greek verb in 5:21 is not *tēreō* (to keep) but *phylassō* (to guard, to keep), the meaning is not significantly altered. We are to keep the true God and to keep ourselves from idols. The NRSV so translates *phylassō* in 5:21. The NABRE's "be on your guard against idols" blurs the antithetical rapport with 5:18b.

tion to forsake the world. Rather, it is an invitation to engage with and within the world, without being subdued by the corrupt logic running it. If the world runs on a logic of covetousness and boastfulness (2:16), we must not be deceived by its lures, for the would-be "spirit" of the world is set against all flesh (4:1–6). The would-be "spirit" of the world brings about not caring for others' needs (3:17–18) and, eventually, hatred, murder, and death (3:12–15). As revealed in God's commandments through Jesus's voice and deeds, to keep faith in God's love and to practice such love as offered in Christ conquers the world (3:23; 4:12, 17; 5:4–5). The world's evil logic is a corrupt scheme that will pass away (2:17a), while God's providential plan for enduring life will remain strong (2:17b).

> We also know that the Son of God has come and has given us discernment to know the one who is true. And we are in the one who is true, in his Son Jesus Christ. He is the true God and eternal life. (1 Jn 5:20)

The final word of assurance vouches for our capacity for discernment (*dianoian*, 5:20b). We are not left clueless before the lies that circulate in the world and that would enslave us to idols.

> When everyone else says that the economy must grow, that we have to protect our assets, close our borders, and care for ourselves first . . .
> When the poor are blamed for their own predicament as if they were all lazy thugs, all four billion of them . . .
> When we are told measures against climate change can wait, or that technology will fix the problem later, without affecting *our* economy . . .
> When we are warned that charity is not good for business, or that we cannot simply give away essential services like food, clothing, housing, and health care . . .

No! We are not without *dianoian*, without intelligence. We hear the lies and do not believe them.

Absolutely nothing is reasonable about a single man being worth $56 billion[13]—no matter how astute or business savvy—while four billion people struggle to survive with less than $7 a day throughout our world.[14] Truth cannot be warped by any fancy, academic, sophisticated, institutionalized, or well-financed ideology. Contrary to what the most outspoken of the world's billionaires might muse upon, *vox populi* is not *vox Dei*.[15]

The people of God have received the divine gift of discernment (5:20) and are anointed to know truth from falsehood (2:26–27), especially when discerning in communion together: "we know" (5:15, 18, 19, 20). The world abuses the relativity of human knowledge to pretend each can follow one's own truth, thereby fending off any attack on worldly claims.[16] While no one can hold absolute knowledge—and our partial knowledge is always situated from a particular perspective, encouraging us to walk in synodality and to listen to each other—God, who is made known through Jesus the Son (5:20), is true. Truth is to be found in God. His reliable witness of Spirit, water, and blood (1:9; 5:6–9) guides us through our walking side by side and our pondering in common, in charity, toward the fullness of life and the joy that we hope to reach in divine fellowship (1:1–4; 5:11, 20).

---

[13] Zoe Kleinman, "Is Elon Musk Worth His $56bn Tesla Pay Package?," BBC News, June 14, 2024.

[14] United Nations, "Ending Poverty," accessed December 7, 2024, un.org.

[15] Elon Musk is quoted saying this to justify his ambitious financial package bid; see Kleinman, "Is Elon Musk Worth His $56bn Tesla Pay Package?"

[16] Pope Francis reflects on relativism and the counterbalance of faith and love in his 2013 encyclical *Lumen fidei*, nos. 25–26.

Afterword

Ταῦτα ἔγραψα ὑμῖν ἵνα…
I have written these things to you, so that . . .
1 Jn 5:13a

I have written this book out of the conviction that First John can speak to our times. If the letter's use of the word *angelia* (message, proclamation) in 1 Jn 1:5 and 3:11 is the epistolary version of *euangelion* (gospel, good news), the 105 verses of First John may serve as some form of concentrated version or reminder of the Johannine gospel, what the first witnesses heard from the beginning. As such, the epistle is a powerful statement that the good news of Jesus of Nazareth is about life, enduring life (1:2), life that shares livelihood (3:17) and gives life (5:11), not relenting before indifference, hatred, or death (3:14). In this sense, First John deserves a hearing now, at this critical moment in time, when life on Earth is under threat of being greatly diminished and impoverished by the greed of a minority among the human species.

Those of us who call ourselves Christians and who consider ourselves "children of God," forgiven and born anew by the loving power of God (3:1), "anointed" with the word of Christ (2:27) and fortified by the Spirit of truth (4:6), cannot give up on the poor who cry for justice, nor can we forsake other fellow living species on Earth. Our hope is life that endures, the life that was promised us (2:25) by a benevolent Creator, Father to all (2:14). It is a hope that we hold in common, in fellowship with all the living, by stretching an open hand to our neighbors in need (3:17) and by raising our voices for justice on behalf of all living flesh (4:2).

The last word spoken on Earth will not be a lie (4:20; 5:21), some boastful fancy of a fleeting, coveting world (2:16), because the word that we heard from the beginning (1:1) is a word of love (4:7–12), in deed and truth (3:18). And in faith we know (5:15, 18, 19, 20) that the word of God remains forever (2:17).

As we keep our eyes affixed on the one who came by water and blood (5:6), in the flesh (4:2), Jesus Christ, who lay down his life on our behalf (3:16), may we be overwhelmed by God's love for us (4:19). May God's love touch our hearts, cleanse our minds (3:3), renew our boldness (5:14), and send us forth to meet others—especially those whom we have chosen to ignore, to push away or to other out of our lives—so that we may be perfected in love (4:17–18) through the unfearful sharing of our very own livelihood with them (3:17).

May joy resound all over (1:4), when the poor are finally welcome at our table, Earth is healed, and our fellowship with the living is thus made whole.

> Rodolfo Felices Luna
> San Antonio, Texas
>
> December 12, 2024
> Feast of Our Lady of Guadalupe
> Rose of the Americas, Mother of the Poor

The Literary Structure of 1 John

First John is notoriously difficult to outline. Aside from the author's occasional remarks on "writing these things to you" (1:4; 2:1, 7–8, 12–14, 21, 26; 5:13), unevenly spread, the letter does not formalize with the expected markings of the genre: no name for addresser or addressees, no location for either, no specific circumstance that motivates the communication, no greeting of others or travel plans, and so forth. The letter's vocabulary, although put to use with high symbolic value, is very limited and thus repetitive, blurring the seams between the sections of the writing. One never knows where to pause and wrap up a given topic, since no headings, paragraphs, indentation, or even spaces between words were provided in ancient copies. The so-called spiral of Johannine style apparently connects all concepts in a continuous stream of consciousness.

Given this state of affairs, many modern scholars capitulate or dismiss literary structure as irrelevant to map the train of thought in First John. They propose tentative outlines but stop short of claiming to trace a literary structure. In order to comment adequately on topics relevant to the ecojustice quest, I have attempted first to trace the train of thought through parallelisms found in each section or chapter of this book. Each section was delineated through lexical *inclusio*, and the parallelisms found within each section were also substantiated by verbal recurrences, not merely by abstractly perceived connections.

At the beginning of chapter 2, I provided the reasons for dividing the body of the letter (1:5–5:21) into two main parts (1:5–3:10 and 3:11–5:21), starting in 1:5 and 3:11, with a verbal reprise of the preamble (1:1–4). I also mentioned that each part was made of four sections. Although for the purpose of this book I have dealt with each section separately, one per chapter, they do respond to each other in a chiastic pattern, also substantiated through lexical correspondence. Each main part provides one cycle of the Johannine spiral, yielding the following structure: Preamble, Part I (ABB′A′), Part II (CDD′C′). As noted at the beginning of chapter 6, the second cycle does not deal with different topics altogether but goes deeper in intimately connecting faith and love. It is a deepening spiral to the heart of God's love for us, manifested in Christ.

This is not the place to argue every single parallelism or even simply the overall structure, much less the methodology. The task was done in dialog with a full breadth of scholars in my dissertation monograph, published in 2010 in French.[1] For the benefit of an English readership, I only provide here the sketch of the literary structure found and the lexical recurrences that support it. Again, for the benefit of a nonscholarly readership, I translate the structural markers from Greek into English. I imagine the heuristic value of the outline will be appreciated, based on words actually found in the text; the parallel sections should be evident. At the very least, I hope to challenge the common assumption that no clear structure is discernible in First John. Though spiraling, Johannine thought does not run unbridled; it rather moves through distinctively traceable steps, connecting specific topics through the use of recurring vocabulary.

---

[1] Rodolfo Felices Luna, *Voici le message. La structure littéraire au service de l'annonce dans la Première épître de Jean*, Sciences bibliques 21 (Médiaspaul, 2010).

I have left each part and section unlabeled. Perception or wording of themes may be subjective; evidence of recurring vocabulary is not. I have advanced an ecojustice reading of the letter in this book, labeling chapters; I rest my case on the word mapping of the letter itself.

Structural Markers for the Main Parts of the Letter

Preamble (1:1-4)	
What was from the beginning (1:1a) What we have heard (1:1b, 3b) We proclaim to you (1:2d, 3c)	
Part 1 (1:5-3:10)	**Part 2 (3:11-5:21)**
And this is the message that we have heard from him and proclaim to you that	For this is the message that you have heard from the beginning that

Structural Markers
for Part 1 (1:5 – 3:10)

(1:5-2:7) A ↓	(2:29-3:10) A'
He is faithful and just (1:9) Jesus the Anointed, the Just (2:1)	He is just (2:29; 3:7b) The one who does justice (2:29; 3:7b)
We do not do the truth (1:6)	The one who does not do justice (3:10)
Purifies us (1:7, 9)	Purify themselves (3:3) "That one" is pure (3:3)
Sin (1:7, 8, 9; 2:2) To sin (1:10; 2:1)	Sin (3:4, 5, 8a, 9) To sin (3:6, 8a, 9)
Injustice (1:9)	Iniquity (3:4)
So that he forgives us our sins (1:9)	In order that he took away sins (3:5)
This is how we know (2:3, 5)	This is how are revealed (3:10)
Just as "that one" (2:6)	Just as "that one" (3:3, 7)

(2:8-17) B →	(2:18-28) B' ↑
I wrote to you (2:14) I write to you (2:8, 12, 13)	I wrote to you (2:21, 26)
The word of God remains in you (2:14)	What you heard [. . .] let it remain in you (2:24) If what you heard [. . .] remains in you (2:24)
That which is true (2:8)	It is true (2:27) Lie (2:21, 27)
Up to now (2:9)	So now (2:18, 28)
To remain (2:10, 14, 17) He is going (2:11)	To remain (2:19, 24, 27, 28) They went out (2:19)
Remains for eternity (2:17)	Eternal life (2:27)

Structural Markers
for Part 2 (3:11–5:21)

(3:11-23) C↓	(5:11-21) C'
Belonged to the evil one (3:12) His own works were evil (3:12) Righteous (3:12) From death (3:14) In death (3:14) Life (3:14) Eternal life (3:15) Does not have eternal life (3:15)	The evil one (5:18) Lies under the power of the evil one (5:19) Unrighteousness (5:17) Unto death (5:16, 17) Life (5:11,12) Eternal life (5:11, 13, 20) Does not have life (5:12) Has life (5:12) You have eternal life (5:13)
If someone... sees a brother (3:17) We have confidence in God (3:21) Before him (3:19, 22) Whatever we ask (3:22)	If anyone sees his brother (5:16) We have this confidence in him (5:14) Whatever we ask (5:15) Ask (5:14,15,16) What we have asked (5:15) Pray (5:16)
We know (3:14) You know (3:15)	We know (5:18, 19, 20) You may know (5:13)

The Literary Structure of 1 John

(3:24 – 4:13) D→	(4:14 – 5:10) D'↑
Remain in him and he in them (3:24)	God remains in him and he in God (4:15)
God remains in us (4:12)	Whoever remains in love remains in God and God in him 4:16)
We remain in him and he in us (4:13)	
Spirit (3:24; 4:1, 2, 3, 6, 13)	Spirit (5:6, 8)
Every spirit that acknowledges Jesus Christ (4:2)	Whoever acknowledges that Jesus is the Son of God (4:15)
Every spirit that does not acknowledge Jesus (4:3)	
In the world (4:3, 4)	In this world (4:17)
Conquer (4:4)	Conquer (5:4, 5)
	Conquest (5:4)
God is love (4:8)	God is love (4:16)
God sent his only Son into the world so that we might have life through him (4:9)	The Father sent his Son as Savior of the world (4:14)
God sent his Son (4:10)	
Not that we have loved God (4:10)	I love God (4:20, 21; 5:2)
He loved us (4:10)	He first loved us (4:19)
God so loved us (4:11)	The love God has for us (4:16)
His love is brought to perfection in us (4:12)	In this is love brought to perfection among us (4:17)
	Perfect love (4:18)
	Is not yet perfect in love (4:18)
No one has ever seen God (4:12)	God whom he has not seen (4:20)

Further Reading

Aside from this book, two other volumes comment on Johannine literature from an ecological perspective:

Daly-Denton, Margaret. *John: An Earth Bible Commentary. Supposing Him to Be the Gardener.* T&T Clark, 2017. This is a very well-read discussion of sections of the Fourth Gospel under headings and topics that illustrate an Earth-conscious reading.

Rushton, Kathleen P. *The Cry of the Earth and the Cry of the Poor: Hearing Justice in John's Gospel.* SCM, 2020. The author moves through the lectionary readings that pertain to John, in the order they appear in the Gospel. She conducts a *Lectio Divina* exercise on each of them, from the perspective of the plight of the poor and the plight of the Earth.

If you are interested in learning more how biblical scholars study other books of the Bible from an ecological perspective, the most comprehensive and up-to-date resource is

Marlow, Hilary, and Mark Harris, editors. *The Oxford Handbook of the Bible and Ecology.* Oxford University Press, 2022. Essays by a wide range of scholars on issues, methods, biblical books, themes, and perspectives.

For short, clear introductions to the Johannine letters, I recommend

Carter, Warner. *1, 2, and 3 John: Multiple Readings, Deconstructing Constructions. An Introduction and Study Guide.* T&T Clark Study Guides to the New Testament. T&T Clark, 2024. This is a critical assessment of different approaches to the Johannine letters, very up to date, and committed to the nonpolemical reading launched by Judith M. Lieu.

Moloney, Francis J. *Letters to the Johannine Circle: 1–3 John.* Biblical Studies from the Catholic Biblical Association 2. Paulist, 2020. A crystal-clear presentation of the letters from a mature and well-respected Johannine scholar, inspired by the polemical reading of Raymond E. Brown.

If you are ready for a little more detail, the following are two medium-size commentaries that, although not particularly technical, are well-researched and college-level reads:

Anderson, Kelly, and Daniel Keating. *James, First, Second, and Third John.* Catholic Commentary on Sacred Scripture. Baker Academic, 2017. Written from a Catholic perspective, each section of the letters is connected with the assorted lectionary readings, and Old Testament and New Testament background. Sidebars provide glimpses into related patristic writings and the ongoing tradition of the church.

Parsenios, George L. *First, Second, and Third John.* Paideia Commentaries on the New Testament. Baker Academic, 2014. True to the educational vocation of the series, this volume digests research that illumines the letters, section by section (not verse by verse). Sidebars provide relevant ancient quotes and short explanations, or situate the passage within the rhetorical flow of each letter.

Those hungry to delve deeper and not afraid of a verse-by-verse commentary can benefit from these full-blown exegetical works:

Lieu, Judith M. *I, II, & III John: A Commentary*. New Testament Library. Westminster John Knox, 2008. A nonpolemical, detailed reading of the rhetoric and theological argument in the Johannine letters.

Painter, John. *1, 2, and 3 John*. Sacra Pagina 18. Liturgical, 2002. A rhetorical and historical commentary, from the polemical perspective championed by Raymond E. Brown, and conversant with Judith M. Lieu's alternative approach.

Other commentaries, articles, and technical reads on specific topics may be found in the footnotes of this book. These are not meant to be exhaustive. The wealth of scholarship on the issue is available by consulting each work's sources.

Scripture Index

Old Testament

Genesis
1:1	6n7
1:26	20
1:26–27	20, 102
1:28	20
1:31	99
2:15	89
3	69, 89
3:19	8
3:24	11
4	80
4:9	89
4:10–11	59
6–9	xiii
9:5	102
9:8–11	101
15:2–6	72n6

Exodus
1:8–14	126
3:5	12–13

Deuteronomy
2:31–35	48

Psalms
27:1	30n6
96:11–13	24
98:7–9	24
145:15–17	71

Wisdom
11:24–26	70

Isaiah
60:19–20	30n6
61:1–2	23, 63

Jeremiah
31:15	115

Ezekiel
36:27	94–95

Daniel
12:1	115
12:2	9

New Testament

Matthew
2:18	115
6:28–30	71
9:15	75n10
10:26	33
16:3	58
16:24	128n9

Mark
1:15	57
2:19	75n10
4:22	33
8:34	128n9
13:19–23	55n2
13:22	55n2

Luke
4:18–19	23, 63
5:34	75n10
12:2	33
12:24	71
14:27	128n9
24:51	9

John
1:1	6n7
1:9	31n9
1:10–11	46
1:14	99n6
1:18	83
1:18a	70
1:18b	70
1:51	4

John (cont.)

3:14–15	112
3:16–17	xix, 44, 109
3:19–20	46
3:19a	31n9
3:19bc–20	31n9
3:21	31n9
3:28–30	23
4:10	111
4:10–15	8
4:13–15	111
4:13b–14	111
4:23–24	112
4:24	92n1
4:39–40	xvi
4:42	xvi
5:4	4
6:54–57	112
6:63	92n1
7:37–38	112
7:37–39	111
7:39	112
8:12	30, 39
8:12a	31n9
8:12b	31n9
8:32b	117
8:44bc	73
9:5	31n9, 39
9:22	xvi
10:11	81
10:15	81
10:17	81
10:18	81
12:20–21	xvi
12:24	19
12:29	4
12:31	127
12:31–33	112
12:35ab	31n9
12:35c	31n9
12:36	31n9, 39
12:42	xvi
12–13	19
13:4	81
13:23	5
13:34	31n10
13:37–38	81
14:1–4	9
14:9	70
14:16	37n21
14:18	19
14:20–2	94n3
14:23	94n3
14:26	19
14–16	92n1
14–17	94n3
15:4	94n3
15:9	83
15:9–10	94n3
15:9–11	23
15:9–14	83
15:10a	84
15:10b–11	83
15:12	31n10, 84
15:12–13	81
15:14	84
15:18	46
15:27	31n10
16:2	xvi
16:7–13	37n21
16:21	22
16:23–24	23
17:13	23
17:14–16	46
17:20–23	94n3
17:26	94n3
19:26	5
19:30	112
19:34	112
19:34–35	110
19:35	113
20:2	5
20:12	4
20:17	9
20:31	120–21
21	121
21:7	5
21:20	5
21:24–25	5

Acts

1:9	9
2:33	9
4:16	75n10
4:20	75n10
7:56	9

Scripture Index 149

10:47	75n10	1:2ab	7
25:11	75n10	1:2ad	3, 21
		1:2b	6–7
Romans		1:2c	6–7, 18
1:20	19	1:2cd	7, 22
4:18–22	72n6	1:2d	2, 7, 137
6:1	85	1:3	xvi, 1, 4–5, 124
6–8	58	1:3–4	3
8:19–21	xx	1:3a	3
8:19–22	48, 59	1:3b	18, 137
8:19–23	20	1:3c	6, 14, 23, 137
		1:3cde	23
1 Corinthians		1:3d	6, 16, 22
7:29–31	47	1:3de	6, 12, 14–15, 18
10:11	58	1:3e	7, 22, 27n1
10:21	75n10	1:4	xxii–2, 4–6, 21–25,
12:3	95, 103		84, 134–35
15	9	1:5	3, 26–27, 29–30, 32,
			39, 48, 70, 98, 110,
2 Thessalonians			122, 133, 136
2:1–12	55n2	1:5–2:7	26–27, 66, 73, 138
		1:5–3:10	29, 66, 136–38
2 Timothy		1:5–5:21	136
3:1–9	55n2	1:5–7	22
		1:5a	79
James		1:5b	73, 79
1:17	30n6, 39	1:6	26, 30, 138
2:15–17	18	1:6–7	73
		1:7	22, 26–28, 30–31,
1 Peter			70, 79, 130, 138
3:15b	60n10	1:7–2:2	23
		1:7a	32
2 Peter		1:7b	30
2:1–17	55n2	1:7c	30
		1:8	26, 30, 33, 69n4, 73,
1 John			127, 138
1:1	1, 3, 12, 98, 122, 134	1:8–10	74, 76
1:1–2	106, 121	1:9	26, 28–29, 34, 70, 73,
1:1–3	15, 70		127, 132, 138
1:1–4	1, 47, 132, 136–37	1:10	26, 30, 33, 69n4, 73,
1:1a	2, 6, 137		75, 127, 138
1:1b	137	2:1	26, 34–35, 37n21, 70,
1:1bcde	6, 18		124, 135, 138
1:1f	ix, 6, 10	2:1–2	xxi, 30, 73, 129
1:2	ix, 1, 3–4, 10, 12,	2:1b	73
	87, 133	2:2	27, 31n11, 35, 44, 86,
1:2–3	3		126, 138
1:2a	2, 6	2:3	27, 30, 138

Scripture Index

1 John *(cont.)*

2:3–4	130
2:4	23, 27, 30, 122, 126
2:5	27, 30, 122, 130, 138
2:6	22, 27–28, 30, 37, 69–70, 75, 79, 87, 130, 138
2:7	27, 29, 31, 39, 126
2:7–8	135
2:8	38, 43n8, 139
2:8-17	139
2:8–17	38–39, 66, 79
2:8a	39
2:8b	39
2:8c	39–40, 43, 48, 51
2:8d	48, 51
2:9	23, 38, 41, 139
2:9–11	40, 42–43
2:10	38, 41, 126, 139
2:11	23, 38, 41, 139
2:12	38, 40–42, 139
2:12–13	41–43
2:12–14	xviii, 3, 41, 43, 135
2:12b	42
2:13	38, 41–42, 139
2:13a	40
2:13b	40
2:14	39, 41–43, 134, 139
2:14a	40
2:14d	40
2:15	39, 42, 44, 127–28
2:15–16	42–43, 123n4
2:15–17	xix–xx, 79
2:16	23, 39, 43–44, 46, 48, 187, 99, 127, 131, 134
2:16–17	125
2:17	39–40, 43n8, 88, 134, 139
2:17a	40, 43, 47–48, 51, 131
2:17b	43, 47, 51, 131
2:18	53, 55n2, 57, 139
2:18–19	55–56, 59, 98, 110, 123n3, 125
2:18–20	xvii
2:18-28	139
2:18–28	53–54, 66
2:18ad	54, 58–59
2:18b	54
2:18c	54–55
2:19	53, 55, 139
2:19a	55
2:20	53
2:20–21	56
2:21	3, 53, 64, 135, 139
2:22	53, 64, 123n3, 127
2:22–23	56, 98, 110, 126
2:23	53, 63
2:24	53, 64, 122, 139
2:24–25	56
2:25	x, 54, 57, 63–64, 129, 133
2:26	3, 54, 56, 64, 122, 135, 139
2:26–27	56, 132
2:27	54, 56, 63, 122, 133, 139
2:27d	55
2:28	54–55, 57, 64, 139
2:28–3:3	128
2:28a	54–55
2:28b	54
2:28c	54
2:29	28–29, 65, 67, 70, 138
2:29–3:3	129
2:29–3:10	66, 76, 138
2:29b	67, 72
3:1	65, 67, 122, 133
3:1–2	15, 23
3:1–3	129
3:1a	72
3:1b	72
3:1d	70
3:2	65, 68, 72
3:2–6	67
3:3	65, 68, 70, 72–73, 127, 134, 138
3:4	65, 68, 74–75, 126, 138
3:5	65, 138
3:5–6	75
3:5–9	74
3:5a	68, 76
3:5b	68, 70, 73, 76
3:6	65, 68, 70, 76, 138
3:6–9	75

Scripture Index 151

3:6a	74	3:18	18, 23, 79–80, 87, 110, 115, 134
3:7	65, 77, 79, 128, 138	3:19	79, 140
3:7–9	67	3:19–22	81, 128–29
3:7a	68, 72–73, 122	3:20	79
3:7b	68, 72–73, 138	3:21	79, 140
3:7c	70	3:22	79, 130, 140
3:8	66, 73	3:23	79–80, 131
3:8a	68, 138	3:24	28, 80n1, 91, 93–94, 101, 130, 141
3:8b	68, 73, 76	3:24–4:13	80n1, 92, 141
3:8b–9	75	4:1	xix, 80n1, 91–93, 110, 122, 125, 127, 141
3:8c	74	4:1–6	92–93, 95–96, 98, 122, 131
3:9	66, 68–69, 74–76, 138	4:1c	98
3:9b	130	4:2	91, 134, 141
3:9c	75	4:2–3	95, 110, 113, 123n3, 125
3:10	66, 69, 73, 138	4:2b	99
3:10ab	67	4:3	55n2, 91–92, 141
3:10c	67	4:3–5	110
3:11	3, 28, 78, 80, 98, 110, 122, 133, 136	4:3bc	98
3:11–12a	80	4:4	xix, 91, 141
3:11–23	79, 93, 140	4:4–5	123n4
3:11–5:21	93, 136–37, 140	4:4–6	95
3:11a	79	4:5	xix, 91, 98, 125–26
3:11b	79	4:6	91, 110, 125, 133, 141
3:12	23, 78, 87, 140	4:6c	92n1, 100, 122
3:12–15	131	4:7	92–93, 97, 103
3:12a	80	4:7–12	134
3:12b–15	80	4:7–21	109
3:13	xix, 46, 78, 88	4:7–8	102, 117
3:13–15	124	4:8	28, 92–93, 97, 103, 111, 141
3:14	78, 87, 127, 133, 140	4:8–10	122
3:14–15	124n4	4:9	xx, 44, 92, 100, 103, 141
3:14–17	123n4	4:9–12	93, 95–96
3:15	23, 78, 88, 140	4:9b	96
3:15–16	100	4:10	31n11, 92, 100, 103, 116, 127, 141
3:16	22, 28, 31n11, 69, 75, 78–79, 81–82, 110, 313, 122, 134	4:10–12	83
3:16a	82, 87	4:11	92–93, 141
3:16ab	81	4:11–12	117
3:16b	82	4:12	92, 103, 131, 141
3:17	23, 78, 81n2, 84–85, 87, 110, 133–34, 140	4:12a	70
3:17–18	xvii, xxi, 125, 127, 131		
3:17–22	80		
3:17c	87		

1 John (cont.)

4:13	28, 92–94, 101, 141
4:13–16	3
4:14	xx, 44, 104, 106, 108–9, 141
4:14–16	107
4:14–5:10	105–6, 121, 141
4:15	104, 141
4:15a	109
4:16	28, 104, 118, 122, 141
4:16a	109
4:17	104, 131, 141
4:17–18	108, 128, 134
4:17–19	118
4:17–21	108–9
4:18	104, 141
4:19	104, 108, 134, 141
4:20	104, 127, 134, 141
4:20–21	xviii, xxi
4:21	93n2, 104, 141
5:1	105, 109
5:1–3	109
5:1–5	108–9
5:2	105, 141
5:3	105, 130
5:4	93n2, 105, 109, 117, 141
5:4–5	xix, 131
5:5	93n2, 105, 109, 141
5:5b	109
5:6	105, 108–9, 126, 134, 141
5:6–10	107
5:6–11	106
5:6–8	28, 107
5:6–9	127, 132
5:6b	110
5:7	105
5:7–9	113
5:8	105, 141
5:9	105
5:9–10	107
5:10	105, 113, 121, 127
5:10a	109
5:11	119, 121, 132–33, 140
5:11–12	121
5:11–13	122
5:11–21	119–21, 140
5:12	119, 140
5:13	x, 3, 119–20, 122, 135, 140
5:13–21	120
5:13a	133
5:14	119, 134, 140
5:14–15	123
5:14–21	121
5:15	119, 128, 132, 134, 140
5:15b	128
5:16	119, 140
5:16–17	123–24, 129
5:17	120, 140
5:18	120, 123, 128–30, 132, 134, 140
5:18–21	122
5:18a	129
5:18b	129–30
5:19	xix, 45, 120–22, 124, 128, 130, 132, 134, 140
5:19a	130
5:19b	125, 127, 130
5:20	120–21, 125, 128, 131–32, 134, 140
5:20b	122, 131
5:21	120–22, 124–25, 128, 130, 134

2 John

7	55n2

3 John

6	15n16
9	15n16
10	15n16

Revelation

5	9
21:23	30n6

Index

Abel, 80–81, 89
Abraham, 72n6, 75n11
abuse
  ecological, xiii, 13, 25
  and power, 102
  sexual, 61
adelphos, 40n1
adikia, 74
aggadoth, 80n2
agribusiness, 73, 89n13
aiōnion, 7
alazoneia tou biou, 43n7
anangellomen, 3
angelia, 3–4, 133
angeling, 4
angelos, 3
angels, 3–4. See also cherubim
animism, 101
Anointed, Jesus as, 56, 63, 138
anointing, xvii, 53–54, 56–57, 63–64, 66, 82
anomia, 74–75, 126
anonymity, in Johannine writings, 5n3, 5n5
anthropocentric immanentism, 126n8
anthropocentrism, xx
antichrist, xvi–xvii, 53–55, 57, 64, 91–92, 95–96, 98, 123n3, 125
antichristos, 55n2
aorist, 42, 75
apangellomen, 3
apocalyptic literature, xiii, 47
apostasy, 75
apostolic constitution, 58n5, 58n6
archēs, 2

atonement, 23, 30–31
Attenborough, David, xii$n$6
Augustine of Hippo, x–xi, 76n12, 84, 86
authorship, xv$n$10, 5n3, 5
autos, 75

Bede the Venerable, 76n12
Behrens, William III, 49n12
Beloved Disciple, figure of, 5, 110, 113
Benedict of Nursia, 128n10
Benedict XVI (Pope), xi, 11n10, 21n23, 128n11
Bible versions
  CSB, 31n11
  ESV, 31n11
  KJV, 31n11, 105n1
  NABRE, xxi, 9, 28, 30–31, 42–43, 55n2, 68–69, 81, 129–30
  NIV, 31n11
  NRSV, 31n11, 42–43, 55n2, 57, 130n12
  USCCB, 92n1, 106
biodiversity, xii
bios, 81n2, 87
biosphere, 21, 63, 101, 111
Blosser, Joe, 128n10
boastfulness, xx, 43–46, 48, 79, 88–89, 99, 125, 131
Boff, Leonardo, xiii
brethren, love for, 40, 79, 86, 123n4
Brown, Raymond E., xi, 4n2, 5n4, 55n2, 80n1
Brown, Sherri, 15n16

Index

Cain, 78, 80, 87, 89
Caritas in veritate, 128*n*11
Cartesian thought, 109
Catechism of the Catholic Church, 123*n*3
catechumens, 63
Catholicism, xv, 60–61, 100
charity, xvii, 84–85, 100, 123*n*3, 128*n*11, 131–32
Chernobyl, 36*n*18
cherubim, 11. *See also* angels
chiastic patterns, 136
Christ. *See* Jesus
Christianity
  and the anointed, 56
  apocalyptic outlook of, 47
  degraded form of, 61
  early, 4, 124
  and idolatry, 100
  and paschal mystery, 47
  tenets, 117
  true vs. false, 56
Christian Standard Bible. *See* CSB
Christology, 37*n*21, 57, 95, 99, 108
climate crisis, 13, 35*n*15, 52*n*21, 52*n*23, 58, 72*n*6, 100, 114, 131
Club of Rome, 49*n*12, 52*n*23
Coloe, Mary L., 11*n*9, 15*n*15, 99*n*6
Community of the Beloved Disciple, The, 5*n*4
compassion, xvii–xviii, xxi, 35, 45, 78, 81, 84–85, 110
complicity, 33, 127
concentric structures, 3, 43*n*8
conduplicatio, 42
consumerism, 32, 35, 48–50, 62, 88
COP21 Paris Agreement (2015), xii

COP 29. *See* Twenty-Ninth Conference of the Parties
Corsar, Elizabeth J. B., 56
covetousness (*see also* consumerism), 23, 43, 51, 79, 88–89, 99, 127, 131, 134
cross, 82, 110, 112, 127–28
Cry of the Earth and the Cry of the Poor, The, xiii
CSB, 31*n*11
Culpepper, R. Alan, 5*n*5

Daly-Denton, Margaret, xiii*n*8, 45*n*9
de, 16
Deus Caritas Est, xi
devil, 66, 68–69, 73–74
dianoian, 122, 131–32
Dilemmas and Connections, 1*n*11
Dilexit nos, 118*n*8
disaffiliation, 59–60
discernment, 32, 77, 92*n*1, 94–95, 97–98, 122, 131–32
disengagement, 58, 62, 72, 96, 100, 129
distributio, 42
Docetism, 100*n*7
dokein, 100*n*7
domination, xxi
dualism
  ethical, xx, 34, 40
  ontological, 34
dynamai, 75*n*10

Earth
  biodiversity, xii, 13
  caring for, 63, 103
  depletion of resources, xii, 8, 25, 32–33, 35–36, 48–52, 59, 62, 71, 77, 88
  ecological crisis, xii–xiv, xxi, 8, 13, 25, 31–32, 37, 49, 52, 58

and eternal life, 8–9, 12–13
Gaia theory, 52
as God's gift, 113
indifference toward, 62
and lawlessness, 77
natural capacity of, 13, 49–50, 131
overpopulation, 50
relation with biological life, 8, 10, 13, 21, 101–2
Earth Overshoot Day, 50n17
ecojustice, 135, 137
ecological crisis
   Gaia theory, 52
   natural resources, xxi, 8, 25, 49
   and poverty, xiii–xiv, xxi, 19, 23n26, 29, 31–32, 37
   rising temperatures, xi–xii, 58
ecosystems, xii, 52n21, 58, 71, 88–89
ecotheology, xxi, 48n10
egrapsa, 42
ekeinos, 69, 75
ekklēsia, 15n16
eklektē kyria, 15n16
Eluvathingal, Frederick D., 80n2
encyclical letters, xi, xiv, 87n12, 100, 118n8
end times, 54–55, 95n4
enduring life, 11–12, 14–16, 63–64, 80–82, 87, 121–22
English Standard Version. *See* ESV
environmental sensitivity, 101
ephanerōthē, 3, 21
Epistles of John, The, 4n2, 55n2, 123n3
epistolary fiction, 1-3 John as, 56
epithymia, 43n6
ESV, 31n11
eternal life
   defining, 8–10, 12
   and discernment, 122, 125, 131
   and disengagement, 11
   and Earth, 8–9, 13
   as everlasting, 9
   and faith, 11, 121, 125
   Jesus as, 7, 120–21
   as promise, ix–x
   relational aspect, 11n11
   water imagery, 111–12
etheasametha, 106
euangelion, 4, 133
Eucharist, 108, 113
Evangelii Gaudium, 22n24, 24n27
Evangelium Vitae, 4n2
evangelization, 22n24, 59, 98
evil
   alienation from God, xix, 69
   and apostasy, 75
   and end times, 54
   ethical dualism, xx, 33–34
   and forgiveness, 35n15
evil works, 46, 67
evolution, 19
expiation, 27, 31n11, 44, 86, 92, 116
exploitation
   human, xxi, 48
   of natural resources, xii, 8, 25, 32–33, 35–36, 48–50, 52n21, 59, 62, 71, 77
   as sin, 102
extinction, xii, xx, 10, 52

faith
   and anointing, 56–57
   disaffiliation from, 59–61
   and discernment, 120
   and eternal life, 11, 121, 125
   as light, 37n20
   and love, 21n23, 84, 97, 108–11, 116–18, 136
   as resistance to evil, xix
   shared, xv

temporal perspective of, 9
true vs. false, 96
false messiahs, 55*n*2, 96
false prophets, 91, 95–96, 98, 102, 125
familia Dei, 15
farming, industrial, 89*n*13. *See also* agribusiness
fellowship
  and atonement, 30–31
  and enduring life, 12, 14–15
  expanding, 6, 20–21
  and good news, 27–28
  and justice, 17, 34
  koinos, 14–15, 18
feminist scholarship, 15*n*15
forgiveness, 30–31, 33–35, 117–18, 123, 129
fossil fuels, xii, 49
Fourth Gospel
  Beloved Disciple, 110
  dating, xvi*n*11
  on death of Jesus, 82–83
  and ekklesia, 15*n*16
  vs. First John, 4, 6*n*7, 120–21
  Last Supper, 94*n*3
  Samaritan woman, 8, 111
  women in, 41
Francis (Pope), xiv, 16*n*18, 18*n*20, 24*n*27, 35*n*15, 37*n*20, 51*n*18, 52*n*22, 70, 84, 87*n*12, 100–101, 118*n*8, 126*n*8
Fratelli Tutti, 16*n*18, 18*n*20, 87*n*12
fullness of joy, 21, 25, 46, 84

Gaia theory, 52*n*21
Gaudete et exsultate, 126*n*8
Gaudium et spes, 58*n*6
gender, grammatical, 15*n*15, 41
Generation Z, 61
Genesis, xiii, 69, 80
gennaō, 130

global north, 51, 62, 71, 73
good news, ix–x, 4, 27, 56–58, 63, 133
graphō, 42
Greek
  Septuagint, 9
  texts, xvi, 30, 105*n*1
  verb tenses, 42*n*4

hamartia pros thanaton, 123*n*3
hatred, 23, 40–43, 88, 100
ḥayyê, 9
health care, 17, 85, 131
heaven, xix, 11, 105*n*1
hilasmos, 31*n*11
hina, 5
Holocaust. *See* Shoah
Humanae salutis, 58*n*5
hyper, 82

idolatry, 100, 120–21, 124–28, 130–31
immanentism, 126*n*8
incarnation, 12, 95–97, 100–101, 108, 110
inclusio, 2, 29, 67, 80, 93, 121, 135
indifference, xii, 62, 72, 81, 96
individualism, 86
industrial farming. *See* agribusiness
industrialization, xii
indwelling, spiritual, 94–95
integral ecology, xiv
intercession, 123–24

Jesus
  as Advocate, 37*n*21
  as Anointed, 56, 63, 138
  and antichrists, xvii, 57, 96, 98, 123*n*3, 125
  vs. Cain, 80
  crucifixion, 82, 84, 100–101,

110, 112, 116, 118, 122, 125–28
as defender, 37n21, 129
and Docetism, 100n7
ekeinos, 69, 75
as eternal life, x, 7, 87, 112–14, 120–22, 133
impact of death on followers, 58, 82, 99, 123n3, 126
in Johannine confession of faith, 109–11
and Johannine dissenters, 126
and joy, 23, 83–84
and justice, 30–31, 34–35, 72–73, 79
as mediator, 28
and natural world, 101n8
as outsider, 46
resurrection, 9, 47, 58
reveals God's character, 70
Johannine Comma, 105n1, 108n4
Johannine community
break with synagogue, xvi
dissenters, xvii–xix, 55–56, 98, 100n7, 111, 126
doubts over existence, 55n3
as first audience, xiv–xv, 4–5
schism, xi, xvi–xvii, 53–56, 59
worldview, xx, 46
Johannine community, and oral tradition, xiv–xv
Johannine writings
authorship, xv$n$10, 5n3, 5
concentric structure, 3, 43n8
dating, xvi$n$11
oral delivery, 3–4
John, as Beloved Disciple, 5, 110, 113
John: An Earth Bible Commentary—Supposing Him to Be the Gardener, xiii$n$8
John Paul II (Pope), 4n2
John XXIII (Pope), 58n5

joy
and fellowship, 22–24, 27, 29, 63–64
fullness of, 21, 23, 25, 46, 84, 132
as holy reward, 6, 22–23
Jubilee 2025, 52n22
justice
as Christian duty, 133–34
and disengagement, 72
as divine quality, 28–29, 31, 67
and Jesus, 30–31, 34–35, 72–73, 79
and love, 79, 82
and natural order, 71
and righteousness, 77

kathōs, 69
King James Bible. *See* KJV
kinship, 19–21, 86
KJV, 31n11, 105n1
koinōnia, xvi, 14–15, 18, 20
koinos, 14, 18, 21
kosmos, xix–xx, 45n9
ktisis, xviii, xx

labor pains, as metaphor, 48
Last Supper, 94n3, 113
Latin texts, 105n1
Laudato Si', xiv, 51n18, 100–101
Law, Robert, xi
lawlessness, 65, 68–70, 74–75, 77, 127
Lazy Person's Guide to Saving the World, The, 52n23
Letters of John, The, 30n7
Letter to the Hebrews, 2
lexical clusters, 29
Lieu, Judith M., xi, 31n11, 42
Life on Our Planet, A, xii$n$6, 36n18
literary structure, 135–36

love
  as commandment, 80–81
  and faith, 21n23, 84, 97, 108–11, 116–18, 136
  perfect, 92, 103–4, 108, 117–18, 141
Lovelock, James, 52n21
Love Relationships in the Johannine Tradition, 83n5
Lumen fidei, 35n15, 37n20

Marshall, Ian H., 75n10
martyrdom, 84
martyreō, 106
martyroumen, 106
mass extinction, xii, 52
Meadows, Dennis, 49n12
Meadows, Donella, 49n12
Méndez, Hugo, 56
messiahs, false, 55n2, 96
Millennials, 61
mission, as component of faith, 23, 63–64, 110
Moses, 12
Musk, Elon, 132n15

natural resources, xxi, 8, 25,49
New American Bible: Revised Edition. *See* NABRE
New International Version. *See* NIV
New Revised Standard Version. *See* NRSV
New Testament, ix, xvii, 2, 9, 55n2, 74
NIV, 31n11
NRSV, 31n11, 42–43, 55n2, 57, 130n12

oil industry, 73
ôlām, 9
Old Testament, 9, 95n4
On Care for Our Common Home. *See* Laudato Si'

oral traditions, xiv–xv
overpopulation, 50

paganism, 124
pain, 22, 116
Painter, John, 55n2, 67
pantheism, 101
Paraclete, 92n1
paraenesis, 68, 72
paragetai, 40
Parousia, 55
Parsenios, George L., 81
paschal mystery, 47, 82
pastoral paradigm, 56
patriarchy, xviii
Paul (Apostle), xx, 2, 47, 58, 85, 95, 103
Paul VI (Pope), 58n6
Péguy, Charles, 18
peplērōmenē, 2
perfection, of love, 92, 103–4, 108, 117–18, 141
peripateō, 28, 30
Pew Research Center, 60
Pharaoh, 126
phylassō, 130n12
physis, xviii
polemical readings, xi
pollution, xx, 12–13, 113
polytheism, 124
poverty, xiii–xiv, xvi, xxi, 17, 19, 23n26, 29, 31–32, 37, 85, 111, 131
prayer
  and fellowship, xv, 18, 129
  and forgiveness, 123
  and hypocrisy, 77
  and salvation, 123–24
predation, 89n13, 101–2
pretentious life, xix, 39, 43n6, 43n7
pride in riches, 43n7. *See also* pretentious life
pronouns, xvii, 27n1, 29, 68–69, 75–76

prophets, false, 91, 95–96, 98, 102, 125
propitiation, 31*n*11
prosperity gospel, 125–26
providence, 131
pseudochristoi, 55*n*2
pseudoprophētai, 98
pseustēs, 98
psychē, 81–82, 87
punishment, 104, 118
purification, 73

Rachel, 115
racism, 16
Randers, Jørgen, 49*n*12
Reinventing Prosperity, 52*n*23
rejoicing, 23–25
relativism, 132*n*16
renewable energies, 115
resources
 depleting, xxi, 8, 13, 17, 25, 32, 48–51, 73
 and global conflict, 114–15
 hoarding, 88–89
 and lawlessness, 77
resurrection, 9, 47, 58
Revelation, xiii. *See also* apocalyptic literature
righteousness, 65–68, 70, 72, 77
Rolheiser, Ron, 18*n*20
Ruether, Rosemary Radford, xxi
Rule of St. Benedict, 128*n*10
Rushton, Kathleen P., xiii

salvation
 assurance of, 123–24
 as biblical trope, 30*n*6
 inclusive, xx
salvific reversal, 9
Samaritans, xvi
Samaritan woman, 8–9, 41, 111
sarx, 99*n*6
schism, within Johannine community, xvi–xvii, 54–56, 59

Second John, xv*n*10
Second Vatican Council. *See* Vatican II
Secular Age, A, 61*n*11
secularism, 21*n*23, 52*n*22, 59–61, 72*n*6
Segovia, Fernando F., 83*n*5
self-sufficiency, 86
semitic parallelism, 29–30
Septuagint, 9
Shoah, 115
Simon Peter, 81
sin
 against Earth, 71, 77, 102–3
 Christ as expiation for, 86, 92, 116
 as everyday reality, 33
 and forgiveness, 31*n*11, 33, 123, 129–30
 habitual vs. constant, 75
 and lawlessness, 69–70, 73–75
 mortal vs. venial, 123*n*3
 significance of, 73
sinlessness, 74–75
"sin unto death," 123*n*3
Smalley, Stephen S., 75*n*10
solidarity, 12, 17, 25, 87, 102, 118, 126–28
Solzhenitsyn, Aleksandr, 33
speciesism, 16
sperma theou, 75
Spe Salvi, 11*n*10, 21*n*23
Spes non confundit, 52*n*22
spiral thinking, 3, 135
spiritual indwelling, 94–95
spirituality, 96–97, 100
splanchna, 81*n*2
stewardship, 20
synagogue, Johannine community leaves, xvi
synodality, 95, 132

Taylor, Charles, 61*n*11
temperature, increasing, xi–xii, 52*n*21, 58, 115

tēreō, 129–30
testimony, 2–3, 10, 106–7, 119, 121
Tests of Life, The, xi, 3n1
tetheametha, 106
"that one," 69, 75, 138
theaomai, 106
Third John, xvn10
tithēmi, 81
Torvend, Samuel, 128n10
Trinity, 94n3, 101n8
Twenge, Jean M., 61n12
Twenty-Ninth Conference of the Parties (COP 29), 114

UNEP, 13
UN Framework on Climate Change, 114
United Nations, xii, 16, 35, 52n23
United Nations Environment Programme. *See* UNEP
United States, xiv, 51, 59–61
United States Conference of Catholic Bishops. *See* USCCB
USCCB, 92n1, 106

Vatican II, 58n5, 58n6
vocations, 61–62

water
 and Christ, 105, 107–9, 112–13, 116, 127
 eternal life, 111–13
 pollution of, 113–14
 as source of life, 111, 117
Watson, Duane F., 30n7, 41–43, 56, 67, 80n1, 95n4, 108n4
web of life, 21, 88, 101, 103
wilderness, xii–xiii, xx, 101
wild habitats, xiin6, xii
wildlife, 13, 36, 62, 89
witnessing, 106
word of life, ix, xviii, xxi, 1, 6, 10
worldliness, 40, 43, 67
world order, xix, 47, 66
 zōē, 87
 zōē aiōnios, 8–13, 81n2, 87